OXFORD
Town and Gown

OXFORD

Town and Gown

MARILYN YURDAN

ROBERT HALE · LONDON

© Marilyn Yurdan 1990
First published in Great Britain 1990

Robert Hale Limited
Clerkenwell House
Clerkenwell Green
London EC1R 0HT

British Library Cataloguing in Publication Data

Yurdan, Marilyn
Oxford: town and gown.
1. Oxfordshire. Oxford – Visitors' guides
I. Title
914.25'7404858

ISBN 0-7090-3932-8

The right of Marilyn Yurdan to be identified as
author of this work has been asserted by her
in accordance with the Copyright, Designs and
Patents Act 1988.

Set in Goudy Old Style by
Derek Doyle & Associates, Mold, Clwyd.
Printed in Great Britain by
St Edmundsbury Press Ltd, Bury St Edmunds, Suffolk.
Bound by Hunter & Foulis Ltd.

CONTENTS

ILLUSTRATIONS

Between pages 54 and 55

Between pages 86 and 87

PICTURE CREDITS

BICC: 1. The Sheldonian Theatre: 2. Oxfordshire County Libraries: 5, 24, 26. The Bodleian Library: 7. B. Archer: 8-9, 11, 15-16, 20, 22-3, 25, 30. S. Waldman: 29. Photographed by the author: 3-4, 6, 10, 12, 17-19, 21, 28. From the collection of the author, 13-14, 27.

FOREWORD

Mrs Yurdan starts by posing the question of why Oxford, fairly rich in this respect, needs to have another book written about it. I am not sure that she provides a wholly satisfactory theoretical answer. But she does much better than this. In the course of her short book she provides a very convincing practical one. What she has written is fresh, original in arrangement, and entertainingly informative. She knows Oxford from the core, but she is very good at putting herself in the position of a visitor from outside and explaining without the assumption of prior knowledge. At the same time she provides enough new angles of view and unusual pieces of information to hold the attention of those who know the University well.

She is also particularly interested in putting the University in its geographical setting. It is obviously a national, indeed a world university, but it is also part of the substantial city of Oxford, which is itself set in a still largely rural county. From the time when sixty-three students and about half that number of townspeople once killed each other, to Thomas Hardy's late nineteenth-century Jude the Obscure, who tragically failed to reconcile the slums of Oxford with its dreaming spires, the University and its surroundings were often not on very easy terms with each other. The late twentieth century has brought a better integration, and Mrs Yurdan writes very much in this spirit as befits one who has already written *Oxford and Oxfordshire*.

This book should be equally interesting to inhabitants of, say, Witney, Oxon., who come quite frequently into the city for the errands of daily life, but have rarely encountered the

University, as to visiting academics from Princeton, New Jersey, who feel Oxford is substantially different from their university but do not know quite how or why, or indeed to a sightseeing tourist from Munich or Chicago with general curiosity about Oxford.

The chapter on 'The Ghosts of Oxford' may be treated as optional by those who are not quite as strong on the paranormal as is Mrs Yurdan, and who in any event are not going to spend the night in Oxford.

Roy Jenkins
20 December 1989

INTRODUCTION

Many people will be surprised that a city so world-renowned as Oxford is in need of any introduction. How does the real Oxford compare with that of the myths, legends and anecdotes which have grown up around it over the centuries, though? Does it still deserve its glittering image? The visitor must judge for himself.

It is not unusual to come across visitors, usually from North America, who are under the impression that Oxford and Cambridge are but separate 'colleges', situated within a mile or so of each other, and easily inspected one after the other. The information that this is certainly not the case, and that a three-hour coach journey separates them, causes some consternation, and a serious disruption of 'schedules'. Recently, a seemingly intelligent young American produced a street map of Oxford, and politely asked the whereabouts of Cambridge upon it.

A typical gazetteer entry for Oxford might read:

Oxford: a city in southern England, administrative centre for Oxfordshire, at the confluence of the Rivers Thames and Cherwell, centred on its University. Royal headquarters during the Civil War. Motor vehicle industry. Population about 120,000. London 56½ miles. Stratford upon Avon 39½ miles. Cambridge 80 miles.

The Universities of Oxford and Cambridge, along with more than fifty others, form part of the British higher education system, no more, no less, but they are so often spoken of in the same breath that the word 'Oxbridge' has been coined in order to describe them both at once. On looking up 'Oxbridge' in a dictionary, I was amused, but not surprised, to find:

Oxbridge: a) the British Universities of Oxford and Cambridge, especially considered as ancient and prestigious academic institutions, bastions of privilege and superiority, etc. b) as a modifier, 'Oxbridge arrogance'.

It is the purpose of this book, therefore, to examine the various aspects of the older of these fascinating places, and to attempt to explain something of its prestige and attraction, in other words what separates 'Oxbridge' and more especially Oxford, from other, newer universities.

The book differs from the conventional guidebook in that it seeks to give an idea of what life is like today in Oxford, rather than to deal almost exclusively with the University as an historical institution, and the colleges as ancient monuments. There is a sufficient number of publications of that genre already. Neither is it an 'alternative' prospectus, which aims to lay bare all the secrets and shortcomings of the University.

It is hoped, therefore, to give an insight into what it is like to live and work in this modern city which is also host to a university which has grown up in its centre, and which continues to flourish there like some venerable cuckoo. Discord, and even bloodshed, there has been, admittedly, for it is a love-hate relationship, more than seven centuries old, which exists between Town and Gown.

Apart from Cambridge, no other town, with the possible exception of St Andrews, has had so many years of academic excellence to contend with, so much culture to endure and absorb. Newer industrial cities have managed to envelop their universities so successfully that one can be unaware of their presence, while the more modern foundations tend to be situated at a discreet distance from the heart of city life, thus satisfying the city's craving for the status of university town, without the inconvenience of having students littering up the place. By contrast, in Oxford the two can never be extricated from each other's clutches.

Then there is the Oxbridge college system. This remains one of life's mysteries to the outsider, and causes more than a few problems, both among those who seek to understand it, and those who strive to explain. Both Durham and York universities have colleges, but there are only a handful of them, and they are little more than accommodation for students and departments. Nothing compares, therefore, with the Oxbridge colleges as bastions of tradition, loyalty and fraternity. A student might grumble from the beginning of term until Week Eight about his college, but, let an outsider do so, and he is immediately on the defensive. In addition, Oxford students, even in extreme old age, tend to think of themselves first and foremost as 'Balliol men', for example, rather than 'Oxford men'.

How then, do all the separate colleges fit into the overall working structure of the University? To generalize, the college is responsible for providing a place at the University. Subsequently, it gives the student tutorship, board and lodgings for a sizeable proportion of the time spent 'up' at Oxford, and moral and scholastic advice and support; also available are certain sports and entertainment facilities. In short, the college is a place in which to learn, to put down roots and to meet one's friends.

The University, on the other hand, is responsible for the lectures and departmental facilities, the laboratories, the libraries (although each College will have its own library) and last, but certainly not least, it awards the degrees at the end of it all.

The most apt comparison of the relationship between college and University might be that between the American States and the Federal Government. Whether one is from Delaware or Texas one is of both the State and the country, holding an American, rather than a State passport, just as one holds an Oxford, rather than a college, degree.

It is now time to examine the University and the colleges, the Town and the Gown, in closer detail and, among other things, to follow the career of that mythical beast, the typical undergraduate. First and foremost, though, we must never forget that Oxford was a city long before the University came into being, and has a separate life of its own today.

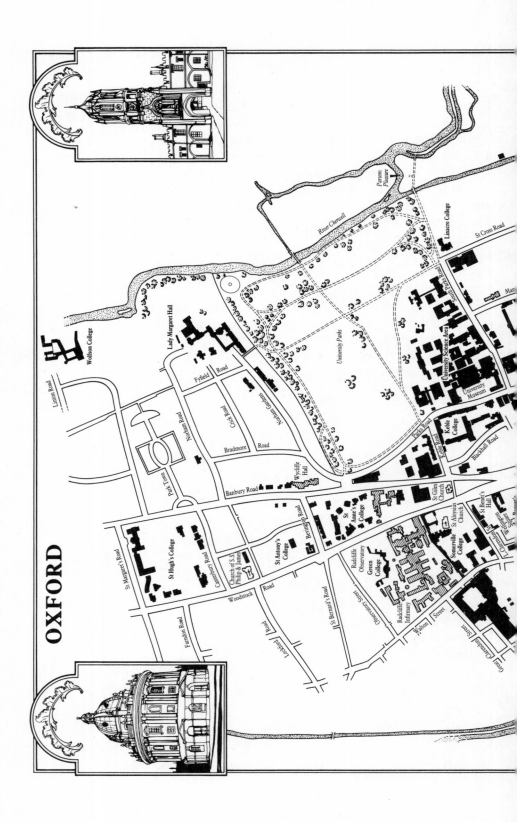

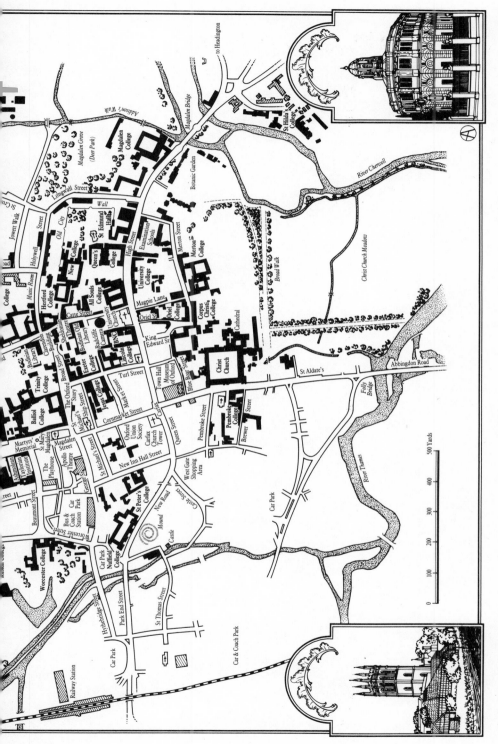

Edanart

Crown copyright reserved

1 AN OUTLINE HISTORY

Home of my Middle Age! Malarial Spot,
Which People call Medeeval (though it's not)
The marshes in the neighbourhood can vie
With Cambridge but the town itself is dry,
And serves to make a kind of Fold or Pen
Wherein to herd a lot of Learned Men.

So wrote Hilaire Belloc, himself a Balliol man, in *A Moral Alphabet* (1899). It is true that the outlying parts of the city, indeed as close to the centre as Christ Church Meadow, are prone to flooding, ready and waiting to give one the sinus and catarrhal disorders for which Oxford is infamous. The reason that the city itself is dry is that it has grown up on a gravel spit.

It seems that what is now the city centre was avoided by the Romans who left their mark in the present suburb of Headington, some three miles away. At some point though, cattle drivers needing to transfer their charges from one bank of the Thames to the other must have had the presence of mind to use the ford near Oxford, and presumably it was these ancient Britons who gave the place its name. Even today the city arms show an ox making its way over wavy lines, which represent water.

It is not until the Anglo-Saxon era, however, that Oxford comes into the light of history. Evidence of Saxon remains, probably eighth-century, were unearthed at Christ Church on the supposed site of St Frideswide's Priory, and seem to confirm the story of Oxford's patron saint. Frideswide was a Saxon princess, who, deciding against marriage, declined the advances of Prince Algar. Undaunted by her refusal, though, the young man made a nuisance of himself by following her around until she sought refuge in Oxford, and founded a nunnery. Even then

Algar persisted, until he was struck blind as a punishment for his unchivalrous ways. Then Frideswide, feeling sorry for him, prayed that his sight might be restored, which, of course, it was. Unfortunately for the romantically minded, nothing further happened to the pair, and the saint continued to live in her nunnery until her death in or around 735.

The first contemporary written evidence for the existence of Oxford is its appearance in the *Anglo-Saxon Chronicle* for the year 912, when it is called 'Oxnaford'. The regular plan of the old streets, still apparent today, is also a sign of Saxon settlement. Saxon work remains in the tower of the Church of St Michael at the North Gate, Oxford's oldest surviving building.

Edward the Confessor was born at Islip nearby, in 1005, and by the time of the Battle of Hastings in 1066, Oxford was a well established centre of commercial activity, and estimated as the sixth largest town in England, according to tax returns.

In 1071 the castle was constructed to serve both as a royal residence and as an administrative centre for the surrounding area. Of this Norman building only a tower and the crypt are left. The castle's claim to fame is that it was the scene of Queen Mathilda's escape from Oxford after she had been beseiged by her rival and cousin, Stephen, during the winter of 1142 when the country was torn by civil war. The castle was used as a prison, and the Assize Court held there, until 1577, when a mysterious outbreak of gaol fever carried off not only the inmates, but also the presiding officials. That year's sessions were known thereafter as the Black Assize.

The twelfth century saw the founding of a number of religious houses, and in 1191 Oxford issued its own charter. It can also boast the birthplace of Richard the Lionheart, and probably his brother, the unpopular John, in Beaumont Palace.

The Middle Ages were a time of marked decline in the fortunes of the city, with the growth of the infant University, which soon became a force to be reckoned with.

Neither Oxford nor Cambridge University was ever formally founded, but the date of origin of the former is generally accepted as being the early twelfth century when, due to a fit of xenophobia in France, foreign students were forced to leave the country. Certainly, in 1167 there was an exodus of British students returning home from France. It is likely that many of them were attracted to Oxford by the fact that it already had a castle, a number of religious foundations, and royal residences both in the town itself and in the surrounding area. Moreover, it was near the centre of the country, at a convenient distance from London, and enjoyed a good system of communications by both road and river, dating back to pre-Roman times.

The behaviour of these new Oxford residents left much to be desired. The students behaved as students in any place and at any time generally behave. The sudden influx of strangers meant an invasion of the townsfolk's privacy, as well as demands on their food supplies and accommodation. Intense jealousy grew up, both of the incoming 'foreigners' suddenly thrust upon them, and of the real aliens who soon came to join them.

'Town and Gown' relations continued to suffer bickering and arguing until, in 1209, a serious riot broke out. Three students were killed by townspeople in revenge for the death of an Oxford woman. Many students fled the town, some going to Cambridge, and, it is believed, creating the nucleus of a new and rival university there.

The remaining Oxford students grew both in strength and in numbers, privileges being granted them in recompense for each attack by Town. The first Chancellor was Robert Grosseteste, Bishop of Lincoln, who encouraged Dominican and Franciscan friars to settle in Oxford in the 1220s. Subsequent bishops continued as Chancellor until the Reformation. Many of the friars were outstanding scholars, in particular the Franciscans who included the famous Roger Bacon.

These early students lived in rented accommodation, halls and private houses, under the command of senior students known as 'masters'. This is the reason why it is impossible to establish with any certainty the date of the beginning of the University; there were no central buildings or administrative system in the early years by which the origin and growth of the student body can be traced.

Gradually, however, came endowments and purpose-built

colleges and halls. During the course of the thirteenth century University, Balliol and Merton colleges were founded; these three continue to vie with each other for the distinction of being the oldest college, but whether one counts buildings, endowments or statutes, who can say with any fairness? Further institutions came into being, many of them disappearing again over the years or being absorbed by their larger and richer neighbours.

The first University, as opposed to college, building, is Congregation House, an early fourteenth-century construction which now forms part of the University Church of St Mary the Virgin. As the fourteenth century progressed, the life of the town declined more and more, and this caused greater tensions than ever. Local opinion grew so anti-clerical that the year 1330 brought another exodus, this time to Stamford in Lincolnshire.

Even this decline in student numbers failed to improve the situation. In the February of 1355, on St Scholastica's day, a most horrendous event occurred, one which was to affect the life of Oxford for the next five centuries. It was nothing less than a massacre, and went down in history as one of the blackest days on record.

Starting with a dispute over the quality of the beer stocked by the Swindlestock Tavern on Carfax, the brawling, pillaging and firing of property continued unabated for two days and nights. At the end of it all, sixty-three students lay dead, and perhaps half that number of townspeople had lost their lives. The king, Edward III, involved himself in the dispute, with the result that a favourable charter was granted to Gown, to the great humiliation and chagrin of Town.

The mayor and burgesses were forced to attend a church service annually in St Mary's, on the anniversary of the massacre, and were to hand over a fine of 1d in recognition of each student slain. This penance continued until 1825 when the mayor rebelled and refused to submit any longer to this centuries-old edict. It is pleasant to relate that in 1955, the six-hundreth anniversary of the massacre, the mayor of the day was given an honorary doctorate as an olive branch.

Sixteenth-century Oxford was a leading centre of the

Renaissance in England. Several colleges arose on the sites of religious foundations which had been suppressed by Henry VIII, and students were no longer required to be in holy orders. The Reformation and Counter-Reformation rocked the country, and resulted in both the dispersement of the books and manuscripts in the University library, and the burning at the stake of the Protestant martyrs Latimer, Ridley and Cranmer under Mary Tudor.

During the Civil Wars of the 1640s, the University was mainly for the King, the city largely Parliamentarian in sympathy. Charles I and his court lodged at Christ Church, his Queen, Henrietta Maria, being accommodated next door at Merton. During the seige of Oxford, Oliver Cromwell had his headquarters on the outskirts. When he became Chancellor of the University during the Protectorate, Cromwell would always stay at All Souls when in Oxford.

In the 1660s Oxford became a second capital once again when the plague ravished London. With Charles II's encouragement, the University produced several outstanding scientists, chief of whom was Wren, whose meetings were destined to develop into the nucleus of the Royal Society.

By contrast, the eighteenth century was a period of stagnation and decline, with corruption rife, as shown in contemporary cartoons. Teaching posts involved little or no responsibility, and students spent much of their time drinking and riding to hounds. In 1800 written examinations were introduced, but apart from this the early years of the nineteenth century saw little improvement.

With Victoria's accession in 1837, though, began a great revival in both morals and learning, with Balliol and Christ Church well to the fore in the production of leading statesmen and divines, as well as educationists.

In mid-century dons were first permitted to marry, and this led to a breakdown of the centuries-old ideal of the all-male Oxford community, and with it the establishment of new, middle-class suburbs, notably in north Oxford.

In 1871 the University finally opened its doors to non-Anglicans, thus paving the way for the arrival of gifted students from all over the world. The first women's college opened in the 1870s, although women were not awarded degrees until 1920. The last decade of the Victorian era was a turning point for Oxford, both University and city, for, in a workshop in Longwall Street, the young William Morris was already making those bicycles which were to be the forerunners of his car industry, the ancestors of Morris Motors, British Leyland and Austin Rover.

Having escaped from the grim clutches of the Vice-Chancellor and his minions, from the curfew and the censor, Town may be said to have stifled Gown to a large extent. The motor car has now taken over the city, both physically and economically, so that the descriptions of Oxford being a city of 'screaming tyres' and the 'Latin Quarter of Cowley' have more than a grain of truth in them.

Other modern industries include the manufacture of scientific and technical instruments, light engineering, publishing, tourism, and, hardly surprisingly, education at all levels.

Modern Oxford appears in a complete range of styles, sights and smells, from the startling and controversial to the careful and loving copies of treasures from the past. The heart and soul, the very essence of Oxford, can be summed up as an intriguing mixture of ancient and modern, of British insularity and influences from every continent. It is, at one and the same time, traditional and revolutionary, scornful and charming, quirky and pernickety.

This bastion of privilege and Britishness has, nevertheless, a noticeable population of West Indian and Asian residents, proper communities, each with its own shops, restaurants, clubs and societies; witness the Afro-Caribbean Cricket Club and the mosque in Bath Street. Besides these and other 'New Commonwealth' Oxonians, there is a quota of Irish and Italians, Spanish and assorted Slavs, Germans, Greeks, Americans, Chinese, Japanese and Vietnamese.

Matthew Arnold's dreaming spires stopped whispering their last enchantments of the Middle Ages soon after William Morris started to make his bicycles, and today. it is much easier to direct American tourists to the Information Centre via McDonald's than it is to send them through Radcliffe Square.

2 THE OXFORD COLLEGES

All Souls College; Balliol College; Brasenose College; Christ Church; Corpus Christi College; Exeter College; Hertford College; Jesus College; Keble College; Lady Margaret Hall; Lincoln College; Magdalen College; Merton College; New College; Oriel College; Pembroke College; The Queen's College; St Anne's College; St Catherine's College; St Edmund Hall; St Hilda's College; St Hugh's College; St John's College; St Peter's College; Somerville College; Trinity College; University College; Wadham College; Worcester College; The Postgraduate Colleges; Permanent Private Halls.

All of the pre-Reformation colleges are situated near each other in the heart of Oxford, and, like the rings in a tree-trunk, one can tell the approximate age of a college by its distance from the centre of the city. It is difficult, however, to divide the colleges accurately into ancient and modern for, as will be seen, many of the Tudor, Stuart and Georgian foundations, are on the sites of medieval halls or colleges which were suppressed after the Reformation, and indeed these newer colleges contain much of their predecessors' fabric, treasures and even customs.

All the colleges are open to visitors at some time or another, but the great difficulty is establishing just when this will be. As a general rule, they will be open from 2 p.m. until 5 p.m. or until dusk, but several, namely Christ Church and the modern colleges, are open all day. Some open earlier during vacations, while some may not open at all for weeks on end, particularly if they have important maintenance or restoration to deal with.

Likewise a college which is normally open every afternoon may close without warning for a wedding or gaudy. If it is important to see one college above all others, it would be sensible to contact the lodge as near to the proposed date of the visit as possible to make sure that it will in fact be open.

While colleges close for a good reason, they may not be averse to allowing in a single visitor or a family as opposed to a party of tourists with a guide. It is always worth asking, but do take no for an answer.

Visitors should remember at all times that the colleges are people's places of work, and even homes, and should be respected as such; to enter them is a privilege, not a right, and staircases are strictly private.

It should be noted that certain colleges charge for admittance.

ALL SOULS COLLEGE

High Street, Oxford OX1 4AL (0865   279379)
Corporate Title: The Warden and College of the Souls of all Faithful People deceased, in the University of Oxford

The college was founded in 1438 by Henry VI and his Archbishop of Canterbury, Henry Chichele (pronounced 'Chitchlee'). It was raised as a memorial to all those who lost their lives in the Hundred Years' War. The King's father, Henry V, with his 'band of brothers' had been the victor of Agincourt. Oliver Cromwell used to lodge at All Souls during his Chancellorship from 1651 to 1657.

All Souls is unique among the older Oxford colleges in that, apart from four Bible Clerks, whom it no longer has, all its members are Fellows. According to an Oxford joke, All Souls men were 'well born, well dressed, and moderately well educated'. This is a twist on the original statutes which required them to be 'de legitimo matrimonio nati, vestiti sicut eorum honestati conventi clericali' and 'in plano cantu competentur docti' meaning that among other requirements, they should be born in wedlock, dressed as befitted their respectable position as clerics, and able to sing plain song adequately. It was indeed necessary for Fellows to have good family connections and a private income, as their fellowships were poorly endowed.

Once, preference was given to founder's kin, unto the tenth generation, but this no longer applies.

The Front Quad of All Souls dates from the middle of the fifteenth century, and has changed little since then. The impress-ive chapel, on the north side, is known for its reredos, covered in figures of saints and bishops. The chapel also has angels on its hammerbeam roof, and carving on its stalls.

Through an archway is Hawksmoor's Great Quad, eighteenth century, and showing the influence of the architect's master, Christopher Wren. In Great Quad is one of Oxford's finest libraries, the Codrington, built by sugar magnate Christopher Codrington in 1756. Among its 150,000 volumes dating from the eleventh century onwards are Wren's designs for St Paul's Cathedral. The library interior has lovely plasterwork, and classical concerts are given in it.

Outside, in the quad, is the Wren sundial; it is assumed to be by Wren, although this has not been proven, for he was Bursar here when it was made in 1658. Nearby is the medieval hall, restored in the late eighteenth century, with portraits of All Souls men, including one of Archbishop Chichele.

One of Oxford's greatest idiosyncrasies is the Ceremony of the Hunting of the Mallard. This takes place every hundred years, on 14 January in the first year of the new century. The Warden as Head of House leads a procession carrying lighted torches, in search of the legendary mallard, said to have flown up out of a drain when the foundations of the college were being dug. If and when they do find it, it will be a very old bird indeed! In the meantime they march around the college singing the Mallard Song, a ditty which is also sung at All Souls gaudies in the intervening years. This must never reach the ears of strangers. The version sung in 1901 went:

> The Griffin, Bustard, Turkey, Capon,
> Let other hungry mortals gape on,
> And on their bones with stomach fall hard,
> 'But let All Souls' men have their Mallard.
>
> *Chorus*: Then let us sing and dance a galliard,
>   To the remembrance of the mallard,

And as the mallard goes in pool,
Let's dabble, duck, and dive in bowl.
Ho the blood of King Edward, by the blood of King Edward,
It was a swapping, swapping, mallard.

The Romans once admired a Gander,
More than they did their best Commander,
Because he saved, if some don't fool us,
The place that's named from the skull of Tolus.

(Chorus)

The poets fained Jove turned a swan,
But let them prove it if they can,
As for our proof it's not at all hard,
He was a swapping, swapping mallard.

(Chorus)

Then let us drink and dance a galliard,
In the remembrance of the mallard,
And as the mallard doth in pool,
Let's dabble, dive, and duck in bowl.

Copied direct from a college history printed in 1901

While all this is going on, the Lord Mallard is carried round in procession seated in a sedan chair, with a dead duck suspended from a pole. They all process three times round the quad, and then proceed up to the roof, still in search of that elusive bird.

Those who live within earshot of all this nocturnal adventuring might be well advised to make arrangements to spend the night of 14 January 2001 away from home!

BALLIOL COLLEGE

Broad Street, Oxford OX1 3BJ (0865   277777)
Corporate Title: Master and Scholars of Balliol College in the University of Oxford.

The foundation of Balliol is curious in that it was the result of a penance imposed upon a Scottish nobleman, John de Balliol, father of a future king of Scotland, after a quarrel with the powerful Bishop of Durham. This was in 1263, which makes Balliol, along with Merton and University colleges, one of the three oldest in Oxford.

Balliol died in 1269, leaving his widow, Dervorguilla, to complete his work at Oxford, and it always remained a project close to her heart.

The College has always had a reputation for scholarship, helping both to encourage the development of the Renaissance in England, and to revive the standards of learning in early Victorian Oxford, after a decline in the eighteenth century. Today it is regarded as somewhat socialist in its political outlook, but nevertheless a good source of University Chancellors.

Apparently, Balliol had a connection with Worcestershire, as, in the seventeenth century, Anthony à Wood wrote of it as being 'commonly known by the name of Worcester College'. This has no bearing upon the present college of that name.

Despite the antiquity of its foundation, Balliol's buildings are mainly Georgian and Victorian, due to remodelling in the eighteenth and nineteenth centuries.

To the north of Front Quad is Butterfield's chapel (1857) which has brass plaques to the memory of former Chancellors, and Tudor and Stuart glass. Other items from the demolished sixteenth-century chapel are the seventeenth-century lectern and pulpit.

Also in Front Quad is the fifteenth-century library, which contains heraldic glass, and houses illuminated manuscripts. Salvin's Tower, by Waterhouse, occupies the north-west corner.

A curious reminder of the bad old days is the Martyrs' Gate, which hangs in a passage in the north-west corner, leading into Garden Quad. It was scorched by the flames when Ridley and Latimer were burned at the stake in Broad Street in 1555.

Balliol's hall, at the north end of Garden Quad and approached by a set of steep steps, was also by Waterhouse, designed in 1877. Beside the usual portraits of Balliol men is an organ paid for by one of the college's great masters, Benjamin Jowett, and intended for use during concerts.

In 1733, during the Encaenia (see page 83) the Terrae Filius, or University buffoon, referred to 'The worthy Head and Men of Balliol (I mean Belial, for I believe it should be so spelt since they are wicked enough to deserve that Title)'. Fortunately, as has already been mentioned, Balliol men were also astute enough to be among the first to pull the University out of its Georgian decay.

Until the 1730s, curiously enough, the college had its own junior Terrae Filius, who would deliver a comic oration of a more or less personal type at an Act Supper which was held in early July. This took place at the college of the most senior of those supplicating for a degree on that occasion. This character, Terrae Filius II, was common enough in the seventeenth century in Oxford colleges, but Balliol men would also bring an oak tree, or part of one, into the hall and place it in the fireplace during the supper. At Balliol this custom continued longer than in the other colleges.

Devorguilla de Balliol

Although it would not be desirable to give even a short biography of all the founders of Oxford colleges, Mrs Balliol deserves a special mention for her loyalty and devotion to both her college and her husband. Her border lord, as we have seen (pages 24–5), quarrelled with the mighty Bishop of Durham, and, as a penance, was committed to maintain sixteen poor scholars at Oxford with 8d a week 'commons' and lodgings which were to be on the site of the present college. John de Balliol died in 1269, and Devorguilla continued these payments in his name, until, in 1282 she presented the college with its charter.

After John's death, his widow had his heart removed, embalmed and placed into a little silver casket which she carried round with her, day and night, for the remaining twenty-one years of her life. The heart sat with her at table, where a place was laid for it and food set before it. After the meal was over, the 'heart's' food was taken out and given to the poor. At length, Devorguilla arranged for the building of a beautiful abbey in her native Galloway, near the River Nith, not far from Dumfries. A

Cistercian foundation, she named it Sweet Heart Abbey, for it was here that she buried her lord's heart, and here too she lies buried near it.

BRASENOSE COLLEGE

Radcliffe Square, Oxford OX1 4AJ (0865   277830)

Corporate Title: The King's Hall and College of Brasenose

'BNC', founded in 1509 by a bishop of Lincoln, William Smyth, and a Cheshire knight, Sir Richard Sutton, occupies the site of nine medieval halls, of which one, Brasenose, can be traced back to the thirteenth century. This strange name comes from an eleventh- or twelfth-century brass door-knocker, shaped like a face with slit eyes and a large nose.

In 1333 the knocker was carried off to Lincolnshire, not to return to Oxford until 1890. It had been at a girls' school which the college purchased in order to regain possession of its Nose. The school was then resold in the 1940s for a substantial profit. The Brazen Nose now has pride of place above the Principal's place at high table, with smaller relatives on view over the doorway in Radcliffe Square, around the High Street doorway, on the college seal, and in its window glass.

Although the High Street entrance has an imposing gate-tower with the Royal Arms over it, entry is by the gate-tower (1516) in Radcliffe Square, and into Old Quad, which has the Tudor hall on its south side. The hall is panelled, with a plaster ceiling, the Stuart arms, and, of course, the Nose. Beyond, in Second Quad, is the fifteenth-century kitchen, the relic of Brasenose hall, and the mid-seventeenth-century chapel, the only one to be built in Oxford during the Commonwealth. In the chapel is a window commemorating the visit of Louis XVIII of France in 1808. His Majesty partook of 'a cold Collation'. The library has about 18,000 volumes in its main section, plus the Hulme History Library and the Stallybrass Memorial Library, a further 4,500 volumes, in memory of a former principal. Off High Street is Sir Thomas Jackson's New Quad, suitably ancient in aspect, with tiny noses around the doorway into High Street.

A seventeenth-century visitor to the college was the 'Child of

Hale' a young giant from Lancashire, whose name lives on in that of the Brasenose boat. The giant was 9 feet 3 inches tall, with a hand which measured 17 by 8½ inches across the palm. Pepys notes in his Diary that he saw what was claimed to be the giant's hand-print during a trip to Oxford in 1668: 'June 9th to Brazen-nose College ... and in the cellar find the hand of the Child of Hales   long' (left blank by Pepys to fill in later). The Child's real name was John Middleton, and he lived in the early part of the seventeenth century. The hand-mark in the buttery is far above ordinary reach. At the end of the eighteenth century his remains were removed from Hale churchyard for fear of grave-robbers, and were kept at Hale hall for some time afterwards.

At one time Brasenose produced 'Ale Verses'. Each Shrove Tuesday, the Butler would present to the Principal some verses written by one of the college students on the subject of Brasenose ale. In return, the Butler received a sum of money. The earliest surviving verses date from 1700, then 1806; they went into print about 1811, and give a good idea of contemporary college life. In 1886 both the Ale Verses and the brew-house were discontinued, although one more set of verses appeared in 1889.

A far more sinister memory is that of the Hell-fire Club, which flourished between 1828 and 1834. Such clubs were not uncommon at this period, and were imitations of the one which met in the caves at West Wycombe, Buckinghamshire, at the end of the previous century.

The Brasenose Hell-fire Club met twice a week, and was not exclusive to that college. The venue was rooms on the left at the foot of staircase VI, which overlooks Brasenose Lane, and is itself overhung by the chestnut tree from Exeter.

The club's activities were brought to an abrupt halt by the death of its President, which was accompanied by delirium tremens, in 1834. Before the official start of the club, however, a woman had died in Brasenose Lane as a result of having accepted a glass of brandy passed out of a college window. This was on 5 December 1827. Both deaths are recorded in the Vice-Principal's Register. The name of the Club President was

Edward Leigh Trafford, and that of the woman Ann Crutchley. The donor of the brandy, H.J. Radcliffe, was rusticated until the next academic year.

These two stories probably helped to give rise to the story of the Devil arriving at BNC, seizing a blaspheming student in his claws, and, having hauled him through the window into the Lane, flying away over the Bodleian with his prey.

In Victorian times, Brasenose was one of the leading colleges of the University; today it is neither important nor insignificant.

CHRIST CHURCH

St Aldate's, Oxford OX1 1DP (0865   276150)

Title: The Dean and Chapter of the Cathedral Church of Christ in Oxford of the Foundation of King Henry the Eighth.

The visitors' entrance is through the Memorial Gardens, and then the turnstile in Meadow Buildings.

Christ Church is often referred to as 'The House', particularly by its own members, in recognition of its Latin name, 'Aedes Christi'. It must never, however, be called Christ Church 'College', for as is the case at Peterhouse, Cambridge, this is very bad form.

Another peculiarity is that those members called 'students' at Christ Church, would be known as 'Fellows' elsewhere, and junior members are often known as 'gentlemen of the house'. These 'gentlemen' number among them many old boys of Eton, Ipswich and Westminster schools.

The original college on the site was Canterbury College, founded by Archbishop Simon Islip in 1363, where Canterbury Quad is now. A more immediate predecessor was founded in 1525 by Cardinal Wolsey, and named Cardinal College after him. It had not been under construction very long, though, when Wolsey's disgrace in 1529 and his death five years later brought things to a halt.

The college was refounded in 1532, and again in 1545, by Henry VIII, this time under the name of Christ Church. The Head of House, the Dean, is unique in that he is appointed by the Crown, and not by members of the college; he is also the head of the Cathedral and its chapter, for the Cathedral is the college chapel (see page 97).

Queen Elizabeth continued this royal interest, and paid the college two visits, one in 1566 and another in 1592, while both Charles I and Charles II lodged there during the Civil War and plague-time respectively.

Those having business with the college or visiting the Cathedral enter by the Fair Gate, which has forty-eight coats of arms to decorate its vaulted roof. Visitors must proceed along St Aldate's, go through the Memorial Gardens, and pay an entrance fee to gain admittance.

Above the Fair Gate is Wren's Tom Tower, a symbol of Oxford world-wide. In its cupola hangs Great Tom, a bell with a chequered history. It once hung in the central tower of the enormous abbey at Osney, which was suppressed by Henry VIII. Tom, however, came to the Cathedral, was rechristened 'Mary', and hung in the steeple. After three abortive attempts at recasting, the present Tom was finally born, and put into his own tower in 1680. The *Gazette* of 9 April 1680 ran an article reporting the event, when 'all the bells of the steeple immediately rang with joy at the birth of their elder brother'. Songs were written about Tom and his brethren: *Hark! The Bonny Christ Church Bells* and *Great Tom is Cast*.

Today, Tom booms out 101 times at 9.05 each evening, once for every one of the original hundred undergraduates (plus an extra one who arrived according to the Thurston bequest of 1663); 9.05 was the time by which they had to be home at night. The extra five minutes is not leeway, but Oxford local time, since the city is west of Greenwich, and Tom keeps Oxford time, not GMT! He also tolls for an hour when a reigning sovereign or the Dean of Christ Church dies.

Once through the gateway, the visitor is in Tom Quad (sixteenth and seventeenth century) one of the largest in Oxbridge, with a lily pond and Mercury fountain in its centre. Tucked away in the corner of the quad is the staircase leading to hall, an impressive example of Gothic revival (or survival) of 1640. Hall is Oxford's largest, measuring 115 by 40 feet, with carved and gilded hammerbeam roof and armorial devices on the bosses. It was completed before Wolsey's fall. The portraits too are spectacular, showing members of the House by old and new masters, a whole series of British prime ministers and other worthies, ruled over by a glowering Henry VIII. Artists include Lely, Kneller, Reynolds, Gainsborough, Lawrence, Millais, Watts and Sutherland. One window in hall has been devoted to a dean's daughter, Alice Liddell, and all her friends from Wonderland and Looking-Glassland.

In 1766 an anatomy school was built to the south of hall, according to Dr Lee's benefaction, at a cost of £2,289. The area acquired the name Skeleton Corner, and the school lasted well into the last century, after which the building became a chemical laboratory.

During excavations in the college in 1783 a real skeleton was found, and was thought to be already five hundred years old, for coins from the reign of Edward I were found nearby. The skeleton had half-boots around its shins, and was assumed to be an early resident of the Canterbury College site. It was reburied in the Cathedral.

A passage in the north-east corner of Tom Quad leads into Peckwater Quad (1714) built in Palladian style, where Peckwater Inn once stood. In the Quad are the college library (1772) open to the public only by prior arrangement. Its treasures include John Evelyn's Diary, plenty of Lewis Carrolliana, and Wolsey's chair and cardinal's hat.

In little Canterbury Quad is the modern picture gallery, which specializes in medieval to seventeenth-century paintings and drawings. One may leave the college through this quad to arrive in Oriel Square.

During the eighteenth century, Christ Church had a curious custom known as 'Burying the Censor'. It took place about Christmas Eve, when there was a Latin speech delivered in hall, and the roll of officers was drawn up for the new year, following the December college audit. The Censor's departure was marked by a recapitulation of his year in office. The speech was written and delivered by a Bachelor of Arts, but the person chosen sometimes backed out of his responsibilities, or messed them up, by giving the speech in an 'indecent and improper manner', which even led to rustication if bad enough. The speeches lasted until 1864, after which they were discontinued.

The 1814, in recognition of the Peace of Paris and the supposed defeat of Napoleon, Christ Church was visited by the Prince Regent, the 'Emperor' of Russia, and the King of Prussia, who had honorary doctorates conferred upon them in the Theatre. The Prince stayed in Christ Church Deanery, the Czar at Merton, and the King at Corpus Christi.

'Prinnie' dined in Hall on 15 June, after which his name was entered into the list of college members, but in 'barbarous Latinity'. It reads 'Regia celsistudo Georgii Principis Walliae Regentis', and the scribe had to have several attempts at it, with 'Georgii' altered from 'Georgius'.

Alice and Company

A little girl, born in 1852 at 19 Deans Yard, Westminster, where her father was Head Master of Westminster School, was baptized Alice Pleasance Liddell, in the Abbey. The Liddell family moved to Oxford four years later, on Dr Liddell's appointment as Dean of Christ Church.

The three Liddell sisters were Lorina Charlotte, Edith, and Alice. They appear in the story which the Dormouse tells at the Mad Hatter's tea party as Elsie (L.C.) Lacie (Alice) and Tillie (Edith's pet name). The Dean's children were allowed to join in the University social life and knew most of the professors and Heads of Houses. They were taken on visits to institutions such as the Bodleian and the University Museum, where the famous Huxley-Wilberforce debate took place when Alice was eight. The girls would have been familiar with John Savery's painting of the Dodo there, as well as its actual remains, a beak and claw, from the Tradescant collections.

One of the children's favourite people was the Maths don C.L. Dodgson, who kept a dressing-room full of clothes for children to be photographed in. He was an accomplished photographer whose favourite subject was children. Even better than dressing up, according to the children, as listening to the stories which he made up, with Alice as heroine. These stories were often composed during boating trips, up to Godstow, down to Iffley, or as far away as day trips to visit their friends, the Harcourts, at Nuneham.

The 4th of July 1862 was a particularly good day in the history of story-telling. The girls and Dodgson set out from Salter's boatyard at Folly Bridge and went up to Godstow. Dodgson continued the story of Alice's adventures down a rabbit-hole, which so impressed the heroine that she asked for it all to be written down at the end of the day.

Many of the people and events in the stories originated in Dodgson Oxford background. For instance, the Dormouse's treacle well, was the well-known Binsey well which the family had often visited, and which was restored by Dodgson's friend the Rev. Thomas Prout in 1857, when he became incumbent. Mavis Batey's book *Alice's Adventures in Oxford*, published by Pitkin, is crammed full of interesting facts and anecdotes about the Liddell family, and the Oxford of their day.

Alice was given the final manuscript of *Alice's Adventures Underground* for a Christmas present 'to a Dear Child' in 1862, but, by the time its sequel *Alice Through the Looking-glass* appeared in 1871, she was a child no longer, but a young woman of twenty-one.

In 1880, Alice married Reginald Hargreaves, who had been up at Christ Church from 1872 to 1878, and they left Oxford to settle in Hampshire. Much later, Dodgson wrote and invited the Hargreaves to visit him once more at Christ Church; this they did, and it was to be a final meeting between them. In 1932, at the age of eighty, Alice was awarded an honorary degree in recognition of her being the inspiration for two literary works. Two years later Alice Hargreaves died, but Alice in Oxford will live on.

CORPUS CHRISTI COLLEGE

Merton Street, Oxford OX1 4JF (0865 276700)
Title: The President and Scholars of Corpus Christi in the University of Oxford.

This, the smallest of the Oxford colleges, was founded in 1517 by Richard Fox, Bishop of Winchester, and confessor to Queen

Catherine of Aragon. The pet name given by Fox to his new foundation was 'our Bee-hive', and, strangely enough, between 1517 and 1648, with the exception of three years, there was always a swarm of bees in the Front Quad. In 1630, when leads were removed from the roofs, a great mass of honey was found there. The bees then swarmed, something unheard of in the college's history, towards the President's garden. In 1633 there were two swarms, some deciding to stay on in the garden, while others returned to their old home in Front Quad.

Corpus's outstanding feature is its sundial, which was designed by Charles Turnbull in 1579–83 and stands in Front Quad. It was restored in 1976, and made accurate once again, giving Oxford local time plus the day of the week of any date in the year, and the dates of the university terms. The sundial is topped by the Corpus pelican, a recent addition by the sculptor Michael Black, who also made the new heads outside the Sheldonian Theatre.

The hall, which is small, has its original hammerbeam roof, panelling and coats of arms. The library, which dates from the early sixteenth century, is endowed with early printed books and classical manuscripts from the tenth century onwards; Corpus enjoys a reputation for producing fine classicists. Book cases have rods to which books would once have been chained.

In the chapel is Bishop Fox's enamelled crozier, and an altarpiece accredited to Rubens, showing the Adoration of the Shepherds. The lectern, with its brass eagle, was given by the first President, and is the only pre-Reformation eagle lectern left in Oxford. A brass to President Claymond is from 1537.

Just beyond the entrance to the chapel is one of Oxford's smallest quadrangles, the cloister-like Fellows' Quad (1706–12). Across Merton Street from the main college is an old student hall, Beam Hall, which Corpus took over in 1553.

Corpus Christi's two principal claims to fame are its old college plate, other colleges having surrendered theirs to Charles I as part of the war effort, and that it is the centre of the Oxford Tortoise Society, which holds a charity Tortoise Fair each Trinity term.

EXETER COLLEGE

Turl Street, Oxford OX1 3DP (0865   279600)
Title: Rector and Scholars of Exeter College in the University of Oxford

Known as the Westcountryman's College because of its foundation by Walter de Stapeldon, Bishop of Exeter, the college has continued to keep up its connections with that part of England. The Bishop founded the college in 1314 as Stapeldon Hall, and was murdered by the London mob twelve years later due to his support of Edward II.

The named Exeter College was adopted in 1586 when it was refounded by Sir William Petrie; between that date and 1404 it had been known as Exeter Hall.

Like those of Balliol, most of Exeter's buildings are now Victorian, the sole medieval survivor being Palmer's Tower (1432), once the gate-house. The hall, built in 1618, with additions from the 1820s, has an unusual roof of Spanish chestnut. The chapel is a copy of the Ste Chapelle in Paris, flèche and all, and is a mid-nineteenth-century replacement by Sir Giles Gilbert Scott of an earlier one. The chapel is known for its Pre-Raphaelite connections, in particular its stained glass windows and the tapestry *The Adoration of the Magi* by Burne-Jones and William Morris, who were undergraduates here. A bad fire in the library in 1709 meant a great loss of books.

Exeter once had a Hell Quad, a small alley which was pulled down in 1855. Heber's Tree reaches across Brasenose Lane and shades the rooms where the future Bishop lodged in BNC.

A new Fellowship has recently been set up at Exeter, thanks to contributions from both Spain and England, under the patronage of Queen Sofià of Spain, and named after her. She was made Honorary Doctor of Civil Law in 1989.

HERTFORD COLLEGE

Catte Street, Oxford OX1 3BW (0865   279400)
Title: Principal, Fellows and Scholars of Hertford College in the University of Oxford.

It is difficult to know whether to classify Hertford as an old

college or a newer one, for it started life as Hart Hall, founded by
Elias de Hertford as long ago as 1284. It became Hertford College
by Royal Charter in 1740, but its statutes were so peculiar that
no-one was willing to become Principal. In 1818 it combined
with Magdalen Hall (not to be confused with Magdalen College)
which burned down four years later, and took over the defunct
Hertford, rechristening it at the same time. Even this was not
successful, and Hertford-Magdalen Hall was reduced to one
student and one half-mad Fellow, with its buildings literally fallen
down around their ears. In 1874, the banker, T.C. Baring,
refounded it yet again, this time with the title of Hertford
College.

Like most other colleges, Hertford incorporated smaller halls
and hostels, one of which was Cat Hall (in Latin 'Aula Murile-
gorum' or 'Mousetakers' Hall'), which stood where the Principal's
Lodging is today. Catte Street is thought to have derived from
these 'Mousetakers', not from any hall, college or chapel
dedicated to St Catherine.

One of the oldest surviving buildings in modern Hertford is the
ancient chapel of Our Lady at Smithgate (1521) where degree
candidates used to pray before going on to the Schools; this is now
the Junior Common Room, and has a carving of the
Annunciation over the doorway. Other sixteenth-century
remains include part of Hart Hall, now used for lectures.

In the South Quad is the old chapel (1716), now the library,
and the new chapel (1908, by Jackson) as well as the late
nineteenth-century hall. Holywell Quad, built in 1977, includes
some seventeenth- and eighteenth-century houses in Holywell
Street.

North and South Quads are joined by Hertford's main attraction, Jackson's 'Bridge of Sighs', built in 1913, and, in fact much
more like the Rialto Bridge.

Visitors are drawn to Hertford by the Oxford of Evelyn Waugh,
as described in *Brideshead Revisited*. Some tour guides even point
out the window from which Sebastian is supposed to have been
sick, but this image of Hertford, even if it were true in the 1920s,
is certainly inaccurate today.

Jesus College

Turl Street, Oxford OX1 3DW (0865   279700)

Title: Principal, Fellows and Scholars of Jesus College within the City and University of Oxford of Queen Elizabeth's Foundation.

Founded in 1571 by Dr Hugh Price, under the patronage of Queen Elizabeth I, Jesus College has always been known as the Welshman's College, because of the nationality of its founder. Today it continues to offer scholarships to students from the Principality, and is the home of the Professor of Celtic. Elizabeth, herself part-Welsh gave timber from the royal forests of Stowe and Shotover. Strangely, there is no mention of Wales in the college's statutes.

For the greater part of its history, until the middle of the last century, when non-Anglicans were finally admitted to the University, Jesus was restricted in its choice of members, as most Welshmen are Nonconformist.

Built on the site of Whytehall and Elm Hall, the oldest part of the fabric is the sixteenth-century Turl Street frontage, through which one reaches Front Quad. Chapel (1621), on the north side, is Gothic in style, with nineteenth-century restoration. On 1 March, St David's Day, a service is held in Welsh. The bronze bust is that of Lawrence of Arabia, an undergraduate at Jesus, and the coat of arms (1693) of a former benefactor and Principal, Sir Leoline Jenkins.

The hall, on the west side of the quad is also seventeenth-century, with portraits of Queen Elizabeth I, Charles I (by Van Dyke), Charles II (attributed to Lely), T.E. Lawrence again and Harold Wilson. An oak screen is carved with monsters remarkably like Welsh dragons.

Inner Quad, with its little gables, took from 1639 to 1713 to finish, and was paid for by donations, largely from Welshmen. To the north lies Third Quad, which was enlarged and remodelled in 1947.

Jesus library once housed a precious copy of *Llyfr Coch* (the Red Book) of Welsh legends and romances, from the fourteenth century, but it is now in the Bodleian Library. Another college treasure is an enormous punch bowl, with a capacity of many gallons; it weighs more than twenty-three pounds.

A sad story is told of Dr Joseph Hoare, Principal between 1768 and 1802. When he was well over ninety he would ride around in a coach, wrapped up to the ears, for fear of draughts, and was generally very careful of his health and safety. Just when the college was beginning to think of him as immortal, although stone deaf, his end came suddenly. It seems he pushed his chair back onto the leg of his old friend Tom Cat. Naturally, Tom hissed and spat and howled, but all to no avail, for the Doctor could not hear his protests. In desperation the cat seized the Principal by his leg, inflicting a nasty wound from which Dr Hoare soon perished. A member of the college composed the following lament:

> Poor Dr Hoare! He is no more!
> Bid Cambria's harp-strings mourn,
> The Head of a House died the death of a mouse,
> And Tom must be hanged in return.

KEBLE COLLEGE
Parks Road, Oxford OX1 3PG (0865   272727)

Keble, opened in 1870 by the Marquis of Salisbury, was the first Oxford college to be founded by the University as opposed to an individual benefactor, and was intended as a memorial to the founder of the Oxford Movement and author of *The Christian Year*, John Keble. Its purpose was to provide university education for men unable to afford it at other colleges.

The college's architecture is of a colour and style which is either loved or hated; few people feel indifferent about Keble. John Ruskin was forced to change his route in the morning to avoid seeing it, but Sir John Betjeman, on the other hand, claims that it is 'by far the best Gothic Revival work in either Oxford or Cambridge'. Also, he thought, 'It is not the product of an antiquarian but of an architect.' Certainly Keble was innovative in breaking away from the old system of rooms leading off staircases and adopting passages. Butterfield's original buildings (1868–82) are an arresting sight: the red brick is interlaced with patterns made by bricks of other colours. The large and rather startling chapel, given by William Gibbs of

Bristol, has, according to Betjeman 'a general effect of wriggling pews, shining brass, mosaics, brickwork, variegated vaulting and soaring marble', which is 'indeed overwhelming'. The hall and library were also given by the Gibbs family.

The highlight of Keble for many visitors is Holman Hunt's painting *The Light of the World*, presented by Mrs Combe, whose husband gave the money to build St Barnabas church in Jericho. The painting is housed in a little side chapel. It is said that because the college charged visitors sixpence to view it, the artist went off in a rage and painted a copy. There are, in fact, two more '*Lights*', one in St Paul's Cathedral and one in Manchester.

Like St Edmund Hall, Keble forgot to alter its statutes to admit women, only realizing the fact in the late 1980s!

LADY MARGARET HALL
Norham Gardens, Oxford OX2 6QA (0865   274300)

Founded in 1878 as Oxford's first academic hall for women, 'L.M.H.' was named in honour of Lady Margaret Beaufort, mother of Henry VII, and foundress of both Christ's and St John's Colleges, Cambridge.

The founding of a women's college met with considerable opposition, and was only accomplished with the untiring support of the Warden of Keble, Dr E.S. Talbot. The first nine students arrived in 1879, under the eye of the first Principal, Miss Elizabeth Wordsworth, who was later to found St Hugh's.

In addition to the original house, further buildings were designed by Champneys, Blomfield, and Sir Giles Gilbert Scott, who created the chapel in the Byzantine style. It houses an Italian painting of the Flagellation, attributed to Taddeo Gaddi, and a Burne-Jones triptych.

Old Girls of L.M.H. include Miss Eleanor Jourdain, co-adventuress with Miss Moberly in their ghostly experience at Versailles (*see* St Hugh's College) and Lady Antonia Fraser.

In 1978, the College's centenary year, it was decided that men should be admitted.

LINCOLN COLLEGE

Turl Street, Oxford OX1 3DR (0865 279800)
Title: Warden, or Rector, and Scholars of the College of the Blessed Mary and All Saints, Lincoln, in the University of Oxford, commonly called Lincoln College.

We are fortunate in being able to see in Lincoln, something of how a medieval Oxford college would have looked; it has been little spoiled by later rebuilding, largely because it was not richly endowed and could not afford continual modernization.

The college was founded in 1427 by a bishop of Lincoln, Richard Fleming, as a stand against what he considered heresies spread by the Lollards and uttered by their 'swinish snouts'. The site was once occupied by the medieval church of St Mildred, and some small halls.

The gateway, with rooms above, and the tower, go back to Fleming's time, and the hall to 1437. The hall has a timbered roof, notable for the only octagonal louvre left in Oxford. Once, all colleges had these turrets to allow smoke to escape from the dining-halls. The roof was rediscovered only in 1889 when the plaster ceiling was removed. In 1699 the fireplace was moved from the centre of the hall to its present place, and the plaster ceiling added. In 1891 the entire hall was given a thorough restoration by Jackson, who also designed the chimney-piece.

The chapel, dating from 1631, has fine woodwork which gives it a pleasant smell of cedar, stained glass by Bernard van Linge, and a carved barrel-vaulted roof with painted coats of arms. The old chapel bell now hangs in Front Quad and is still rung for evensong. A copy of the infamous Lincoln Imp, or 'devil', sits above the doorway which leads to the hall. The bell sounds as a sort of 'almanac', rings steadily for about three minutes, after which it changes to a succession of quick, short rings, then there is a minute's pause, and then one stroke for each day in the month.

One of Lincoln's best-known sons is John Wesley, who obtained a Fellowship here in 1726, after being an undergraduate of Christ Church, and ordination in the Cathedral in 1725. When he married in 1751, he had to resign his Fellowship. The room which he used is between the First and

Second Quads, and has been furnished in his memory, with items which belonged to him on display. Wesley's portrait hangs in Lincoln hall, but the painter is unknown.

The college owns two of Oxford's most famous buildings. The first is 'The Mitre', which features in many stories and novels about Oxford, and was once a coaching inn. Today it is a Berni Inn, with student rooms on its upper floors. The second building, All Saints church (1710) was once the City church, but was converted into the college library in 1975. Rectors of Lincoln were always installed in All Saints and several of them are buried there. The college had jurisdiction over the church until 1866, and a Bidding Prayer is still said for the principal benefactors of Lincoln.

There is a custom recorded at Lincoln, similar to the one at Christ Church known as 'Burying the Censor'; in this case it was 'Drowning the Bursar'. The bursarship used to be an office held for one year only, and when the outgoing Bursar retired he would be 'drowned' in whisky punch (formerly egg flip) with the words 'Bon repos, Bursar'. The same custom was practised when the Sub-Rectors handed their whip of office over to each other at the end of their term of duty.

On Ascension Day the college would turn out to beat the bounds of St Michael's and All Saints' parishes, a custom now retained only by St Michael-at-the-North-Gate. Afterwards, beaters would be entertained in hall with a 'good plain luncheon', and ground-ivy ale, that is, beer in which ground-ivy had been steeped for twenty-four hours. It was also usual to throw pennies down into the Quad, some of them pre-heated in a shovel, for the choir-boys to collect.

The Lincoln Imps

The original Imp, who lives in the Cathedral in Lincoln, arrived upon the east wind, and started making trouble the minute he got there. Firstly he made threats towards the clergy, including the Bishop himself, then, once inside the Cathedral, he tore down tapestries, hacked at the wood-work, smashed candlesticks, and tried to pull out the feathers from the angels' wings. Not surprisingly, they objected and called out, 'O, impious Imp, be ye turned into stone!', and he was, immediately. There he sits to this day, one leg clasped over the other, squatting on a pillar above the Angel Choir.

His relative at Oxford was often referred to as the Lincoln College 'Devil':

> The Devil looking over Lincoln,
> Their faults, be sure, he kindly winks on,
> The other Colleges he squints on,
> A world of pity 'twas, I swear,
> That our young master was not there.

The college Imp appeared in *The Gentleman's Magazine* for 15 September 1731, as the 'famous devil', when he was taken down, having lost his head in a storm two years previously. He was subsequently replaced. This imp was made of lead, and perched in a niche in the tower, facing into the quad. One of the rectors, Edward Tatham (1792–1834) grew tired of lampoons being circulated, in which were mentioned certain similarities between Rector and Devil, and, when one appeared describing how the former returned home 'full of politics, learning, and port' and was seized by the imp and dragged away, Tatham caused the imp to be removed. There is no record, though, of its having been destroyed.

Lincoln Literary Society was christened 'The Goblins' after their imp, who has now been reincarnated in carved form over a doorway leading out of Front Quad.

MAGDALEN COLLEGE

High Street, Oxford OX1 4AU (0865 276000)
Title: The President and Scholars of the College of St Mary Magdalen in the University of Oxford.

In 1458 William of Waynflete, Bishop of Winchester, founded his new college on the site of a hospital dedicated to St John the Baptist, dating from 1231. The remains of this earlier building were excavated in 1987–8, during work on the new kitchens at Magdalen, and showed evidence of a river-wall over six and a half feet thick, and a water-gate, the stones of which have been incorporated into the modern building.

Like its counterpart at Cambridge, Magdalene College, the name of the college is pronounced 'Maudlin', although the Street and Road of the same name in Oxford may be pronounced either this way, or as spelt.

Magdalen's bell-tower, built between 1492 and 1509, is an Oxford landmark, standing sentinel over Magdalen Bridge. Although May Day is celebrated at various points in the city centre it is to Magdalen that the crowds flock at 6 a.m., when the college choir sings its hymn to spring, 'Te Deum Patrem Collimus'. The hymn is said to have been written by a Fellow of Magdalen at the time of the Restoration. Undoubtedly of ancient origin, the hymn-singing would appear to have no connection, as is sometimes suggested, with a pre-Reformation mass said for the soul of Henry VII. Today it is by no means a religious ceremony, and its present form dates only from the mid-nineteenth century.

The entrance from the High Street brings the visitor into St John's Quad; a charge is made for visitors entering the college during the Long Vacation. In the quad is a stone pulpit, half-way up a wall. On the Sunday nearest to St John the Baptist's Day, towards the end of June, a public sermon is preached from this open-air pulpit, on the life and teachings of the Baptist. The pulpit is draped for the occasion with an embroidered velvet cloth, and, on the lawn immediately below, are set the Vice-Chancellor's throne and seats for the Proctors; behind these are chairs for the congregation. Years ago the grass was covered with rushes, branches and meadow-grass to commemorate the Baptist's stay in the wilderness. The sermon was discontinued in the 1760s, but revived in 1896.

To the left of St John's Quad are the Grammar Hall (1614) together with the Victorian New Library and St Swithin's Buildings, and the modern Longwall Quad. The nineteenth-century President's Lodgings lie ahead, and, to the right, Magdalen's original entrance, Founder's Tower, with the entrance to the chapel.

Normally one is allowed only into the ante-chapel, the rest

being visible through wrought-iron railings. There is, nevertheless, plenty to see in the ante-chapel: a fifteenth-century painted
chest, several brasses and the tomb of Richard Patten, William's
father, brought here when the old church at Wainfleet, Lincolnshire, was demolished last century.

Through Muniments Tower is Cloister Quad, fifteenth-
century and decorated with large heraldic beasts called 'hiero-
glyphs', crouching on buttresses. On the south of this quad is hall,
reached by a flight of steps, and boasting fine linenfold panelling,
an oak roof and the usual portrait gallery.

On Corpus Christi Day, in May, a festival usually only
observed by Roman Catholics in Britain, the clergy and choir of
Magdalen College, dressed in their finery and almost pre-
Reformation vestments, process round Cloister Quad bearing
before them the pyx under a canopy. To meet them on their
stately way in the semi-gloom, en route for the chapel, is like
stepping back into the Middle Ages for a minute or two.

Through again from Cloister Quad are the colonnades of the
New Building (1733) with Magdalen Grove, or Deer Park, to the
left. On the other side of the gardens is a small bridge leading to
Addison's Walk, and the Water Walks (see pages 113–14).

One of the college's treasures is its Restoration Cup, used in
hall on 29 May each year. It is engraved with the names of those
college members who came back after being ejected during the
Commonwealth. It is also used on 25 October to celebrate
Magdalen's own restoration, in 1688, of the President and
Fellows who had been turned out by James II the previous year.
When the cup is used, the toast is always 'Jus suum cuique'.

MERTON COLLEGE
Merton Street, Oxford OX1 4JD (0865 276310)
Title: The Warden and Scholars of the House or College of
Scholars of Merton in the University of Oxford.

Merton was founded in 1264 by the Chancellor of England,
Walter de Merton, who is buried in Rochester Cathedral. Later,
in 1284, Cambridge's first college, Peterhouse, adopted Merton's
statutes, and specifically mentions Merton in them, for this was
the first college to build its own premises, former foundations

having used private houses and hostels.

One of the last of these halls to survive, which was finally absorbed by Merton, was St Alban's Hall, had the nickname 'Stubbins', or less complimentary still, the 'Farm Yard' from 'the extraordinary set of sounds which it was capable of producing on festive occasions' (Falconer Madan, *Oxford Outside the Guide Books*).

Merton's Gatehouse Tower (1418) has statues of de Merton and his sovereign, Henry III, together with John the Baptist and assorted carved animals. More carvings, of the signs of the zodiac, appear over the Fitzjames Gateway, above which are the Queens' Rooms used by both Henrietta Maria and Catherine of Braganza in the seventeenth century.

One of Oxford's smallest and most oddly named quads, Mob Quad, is the home of Merton's Old Library (1337–8) which may be visited on a guided tour given by the Verger for a small fee. It is the oldest library in regular use in Europe, and was Oxford's first specially built one, other colleges using an ordinary room for storing books. It is a treasure-house of ancient manuscripts, books and fittings, with a chained volume on display, medieval astrological instruments (including an astrolabe said to have been used by Chaucer), fine stained glass, a thirteenth-century oak chest, and, last but not least, two ghosts.

Something of the atmosphere of medieval libraries is provided by the stained glass in the windows and the lack of electricity. Fortunately for today's students, there is also a convenient newer library with mod. cons. There is more medieval glass in Merton chapel, some of the oldest and finest in Oxford, and monuments to notable Oxonians in the ante-chapel. For a fuller description, see pages 104–5. The hall, which is late thirteenth-century, was redesigned at the end of the eighteenth.

A feature of the Christmas festivities at Merton used to be the election of the Rex Fabarum on 19 November, and these events are recorded in the college Register. This King of the Beans took his name from the medieval custom of making king of the revels the person who found the bean hidden in a slice of cake; however, at Merton, the king was a Senior Fellow who had not already held the title. His duty was to punish all wrongdoing perpetrated over the Christmas period, and his reign lasted until about Candlemas, 2 February, after which came the Ignis Regentium, a wine party which took place round a blazing fire in the college hall, and paid for by the Regent Masters, or Senior Regent.

Anthony à Wood

Born on 17 December 1632 in a house opposite Merton College, Anthony à Wood died there on 29 November 1695. The 'à' was added by himself, and was not used by the rest of his family, or by Wood himself when he writes about them. He wrote both his own autobiography, and journals of hundreds of contemporary Oxford events and characters. Between the years 1891 and 1900, Dr Andrew Clark, Fellow of Lincoln and Vicar of St Michael-at-the-North-Gate, compiled a five-volume edition of Wood's writings, and a small World's Classics edition was published by the Oxford University Press.

Wood was sent to school at Lord Williams's Grammar School, Thame, where he was able to see something of the Civil War at local level. In 1644 he went up to Merton, where he describes his matriculation, and the tricks played on freshmen.

His interests grew to include musical appreciation and playing the violin, but his passion was for old buildings, and the collecting of memorial inscriptions. The happiest days of his life were those spent in the Bodleian Library or poking about in a vault or graveyard. Despite the wicked ways of his home town, which he describes most vividly in all its vice and splendour, Wood was loath to leave it and seldom ventured far afield.

Few people escape his venom on account of real or supposed slights, extending even to Court circles. The Oxford of his day was not dissimilar to our own, and a far cry from the picture of dreaming spires and ivory towers conjured up by Matthew Arnold and Gerard Manley Hopkins. Wood himself was quarrelsome and never in the wrong in his own eyes. He has little good to say of anyone, and yet the way in which it is written often brings a smile. Merton went as far as banning him from the Common Room for his malicious observations of all and sundry. He never married, although there are some veiled and cryptic references to ladies of his acquaintance who would not have him, one, he says, because he was 'full of issues'. He lived in his rooms in Merton Street almost as a recluse, allowing in only favoured bed-makers. He managed to get his book *Athenae Oxonienses* burnt by order of the University in 1693, and, when one reads some of his personal descriptions, it is hardly surprising that those concerned were not flattered. Joseph Godwin, junior Fellow of New College, had, according to Wood, 'a curl'd shag-pate, was squint-ey'd and pur-blind, and much deformed with the small pox'. Nevertheless, a 'handsome maid living in Catstreet poyson'd herself with rats-bane' for love of him.

At the age of sixty-three, Wood suffered a 'total suppression of urine', and, feeling Time's winged chariots drawing near, hurried off to Merton Chapel in order to choose his last resting-place. In his will, made five days before his death, he states his wish to be buried 'deeper than ordinary, under, and as close to the wall [just as you enter in at the north on the left hand] as the place will permit'.

He left all of his manuscripts to the University, to be put into the Bodleian and the (Old) Ashmolean, also all his books were to go to the 'Musaeum'.

NEW COLLEGE

New College Lane, Oxford OX1 3NB (0865   79555)
Title: Warden and Scholars of St Mary College of Winchester in Oxford commonly called New College in Oxford.

New College's title is another Oxford curiosity, this time a double one: firstly, it is one of the oldest colleges, and, secondly, one must always use the word 'College' when referring to it, and not just say 'New'.

New College was founded in 1379 by William of Wykeham, as 'St Mary College in Oxford' to train civil servants, then in short supply after the ravages of the Black Death. Because another St Mary's College, now Oriel, was already in existence, the term 'New' was applied, and has stuck ever since.

The college has changed very little over the last six centuries, and its design became the basis of several later colleges, including King's, Cambridge, as it was originally envisaged by Henry VI.

The New College Lane entrance (1386), with gate-house and statues of the founder and the Virgin Mary, leads into Front Quad. This was the first quadrangle to appear in Oxford. It too dates from 1386, but had an upper storey added in 1675. Fourteen years later than the quad came the cloister, chapel and bell-tower, famous for its series of gargoyles.

The ante-chapel has a whole gallery of medieval brasses, with some of later date, all keeping company with Epstein's statue of *Lazarus Rising from the Dead* and Sir Joshua Reynolds's stained-glass window. For details of the chapel, see page 105.

Up a staircase leading from Front Quad is the oldest hall in the University (1386) with Tudor linenfold panelling and nineteenth-century stained glass with heraldic motifs. To the south of the quad is the Long Room, now used for concerts and exhibitions, but once the college's communal lavatory.

The Holywell Street range of buildings is Victorian, as is the gatehouse, but they fit in well with the medieval parts of the college. The Junior Common Room (1682) is the oldest in Oxford; there was already a Senior Common Room by about 1680. Fines, for breaking JCR rules, were payable in wine; abusive language, for instance resulted in a payment of a dozen bottles of claret.

The New College puddings were once famous enough for a recipe of about the year 1700 to be quoted in books, both contemporary and later. They were made with bread, beef suet, currants, nutmeg, cream and eggs, and were topped by a sauce made of sack, rosewater, and other ingredients. The modern 'college pudding' would seem to be its poor relation.

The members of New College were traditionally exempt from examinations. It has been suggested that they were deemed automatically worth admitting to degrees if they had kept to the founder's rather demanding statutes. This privilege, was, however, voluntarily renounced by Warden Shuttleworth in 1834. Until that date the college had set its own examinations, the first one on record being for a BCL (Bachelor of Civil Law) in 1795, five years before the University brought in compulsory written examinations. When they were introduced, New College men were barred from sitting them, and the college made its own examinations harder in order to keep up the standard. Eventually New College students petitioned to be allowed to sit the University ones instead, but even today the college 'demands' (postulat) degrees instead of supplicating for them (supplicate).

Until the 1830s diners were summoned to hall by two choir-boys who would start by the gatehouse, shouting in unison 'Tempus est vocandi à manger, O seigneurs' with a glorious disregard for the mixture of languages. The call had to last until the boys had reached the kitchen and only then were they permitted to finish their message and draw breath.

The year 1854 saw the end of the rule that only Wykehamists, that is students of the founder's Winchester College, were allowed into New College. There was no College Eight until 1869, as Winchester was not a rowing school and there were no decent oarsmen. One of Oxford's more interesting traditions is a very recent revival of one that was as old as New College itself. In the mid-1980s the then Lord Mayor, Dr Frank Garside, decided to revive the ancient custom of 'Riding the Franchise'. This dates back to 1391 and requires a tour of the city boundaries. The most spectacular aspect of all this was the sight of the Lord Mayor, together with the Vice-Chancellor, mounting the medieval wall in New College in order to inspect its state of repair. This is in accordance with the terms by which the founder was allowed to purchase the site, which stipulated that the fortifications were to be kept in good repair. So conscientiously has this been done by New College that this stretch, along with another in Deadman's Walk, south of Merton, are the only sections of wall to survive, that in New College being complete with a bastion. The Lord Mayor's inspection now takes place every three years.

ORIEL COLLEGE

Oriel Street, Oxford OX1 4EW (0865   276555)
Title: The Provost and Scholars of the House of the Blessed Mary the Virgin in Oxford, commonly called Oriel College, of the

Foundation of Edward the Second of famous memory, sometime King of England. Founded as St Mary's College, Oriel took its present name from a large and decorative window in a house belonging to the Crown called La Oriole. The first founder, in 1324, was Adam de Brome, almoner to Edward II, and also rector of St Mary the Virgin church. Apart from La Oriole, several small houses and halls were on the site.

Two years later the King himself refounded the college, making it Oxford's first royal foundation by giving it St Mary's Hall (nicknamed 'Skimmery'). The Rhodes building occupies part of its site today, north of the main part of the college. St Mary's Hall was finally incorporated with Oriel in 1902, and forms the oldest part of it, for none of the other Oriel buildings are medieval.

On entering the college, the visitor is struck by the front porch which has two canopies with statues of the founder, Edward II, and of Charles I. Above them are the Virgin and Child, under a second canopy. The steps leading up to the porch go to the hall, built at the start of the Civil War, and possessing a hammerbeam roof. Oriel chapel also dates from 1642. In Back Quad is Wyatt's fine library.

The college saw the birth of the Oxford, or Tractarian, Movement, in its Senior Common Room in the 1830s, and a former member of Oriel was Cecil Rhodes, who endowed the Rhodes Scholarship and gave the money for the Rhodes Building which forms Oriel's High Street frontage. It is of seventeenth-century style, by Champneys, and has a statue of Rhodes.

Oriel was the last men's college to admit women, protesting to the end that, apart from the inconvenience of having to build new lavatories, the college's rowing standards would drop. In the mid-1980s, a medieval privy was unearthed in the Provost's Lodgings, and samples of its contents taken away for analysis in order to discover more about what our ancestors ate.

Oriel owns what is claimed to be Oxford's oldest existing student accommodation. This is Tackley's Inn, which dates from 1326, and has a ground floor basement leased out to the Abbey National Building Society and the Royal Bank of

Scotland. Oriel began restoration work in 1986, employing no architects, but only members of the college. On the first floor, existing kitchens have been removed and a fourteenth-century chimney uncovered. On the middle floor, the medieval chamber has been re-created by the removal of partitions. In addition, twelve student rooms have been made. All through the inn there has been a policy of exposing and repointing the stone walls, and five sixteenth-century fireplaces have been uncovered. Oriel plans to continue with similar restoration work on buildings which it owns on the 'Island site' all round Tackley's Inn, across Oriel Street from the college itself.

PEMBROKE COLLEGE

Pembroke Square, off St Aldate's, Oxford OX1 1DW (0865 276444)

Title: The Master, Fellows, and Scholars of Pembroke College in the University of Oxford.

Claiming James I and VI as its Founder, the College takes its name from William Herbert, Earl of Pembroke, and Chancellor of the University at the time of its foundation in 1624. It keeps a close link with Abingdon School (formerly Roysse's) thanks to endowments from Thomas Tesdale of Abingdon, who, with Richard Wightwick, put up the money for Pembroke's foundation.

A predecessor, Broadgates Hall, known for its production of lawyers, was absorbed by Pembroke, members of Broadgates automatically becoming members of Pembroke. Today, all that is left of the hall is in the Senior Common Room to the right of Front Quad.

The early eighteenth-century chapel, which was renovated in 1973, has late nineteenth-century glass showing James I and Charles I. The dining hall (1847) has a portrait gallery, including one by Kneller of Queen Anne. The traditional signal for saying grace is three blows with two wooden trenchers, such as were used in Hall until 1848, upon the wooden table.

Pembroke has found good friends in several generations of the McGowin family from Alabama, who provided the money for a new library (1974) and other amenities. The Wolfson

Foundation, whose gifts are to be found all over Oxford and Cambridge, provided the Macmillan Building, which was finished in 1977 and is used for undergraduate accommodation. It was named after the Chancellor at the time, Harold Macmillan, Earl of Stockton.

Pembroke's favourite son, whose enormous Worcester teapot and cider-mug it still treasures, did not stay there long enough to take his degree, because of lack of funds. He was Samuel Johnson, of dictionary fame, a Lichfield boy who was, at times, too poor to afford shoes. Later he was awarded an honorary MA in place of the BA which he could not take, and he held back the publication of his dictionary until he could place 'MA' after his name. His bust, by Bacon, is in the library.

At Pembroke, a servitor was employed by the Master as a sort of informant, whose duty it was to knock at the doors of undergraduates' rooms to find out if the inmate was at home; if he was out, his name was reported to the Master. This practice was seen as an invasion of privacy, and the servitor would be set upon and chased downstairs with blows from pots and candlesticks by junior members, including the young Samuel Johnson.

Entries in the Bursars' accounts under the heading 'pro ostreis' relate to the Pembroke annual Oyster Feast, now no longer held.

THE QUEEN'S COLLEGE
High Street, Oxford OX1 4AW (0865   279120)
Title: The Provost and Scholars of the Queen's College in the University of Oxford.

The Queen in question is Philippa of Hainault, wife of Edward III; the college was founded by her chaplain Robert de Eglesfield in 1340. The position of the apostrophe in the college's title is important, distinguishing it from Queens', Cambridge, which had two founders. Today, Queen Elizabeth the Queen Mother is the college Patroness. Despite being such an ancient foundation, Queen's is another college which retains none of its medieval buildings, the oldest being seventeenth-century.

The college has always kept close ties with Cumbria and the

north of England generally, as de Eglesfield was a Cumberland man. Because of the distance which these early students were from their homes in the north, they would stay in Oxford for Christmas and New Year, and Queen's still continues its traditional seasonal entertainments, namely the Boar's Head Dinner and the Needle and Thread ceremony. Also, according to the founder's command, college members are called to dinner by trumpet, and his mounted horn is still used at gaudies as a loving-cup.

The Boar's Head ceremony is said to have its origins in the adventures of a medieval scholar at Queen's who was startled by a wild boar while studying in a nearby forest. Fearlessly he thrust his volume of Aristotle down the creature's throat, exclaiming 'Graecum est!' The boar choked on the learned tome and gave up the ghost immediately. The enterprising young man cut off its head and brought it triumphantly back to college where it was served up for dinner in hall. Today, at Christmas, a boar's head, garlanded and with an orange in its mouth, is carried into hall to the accompaniment of the *Boar's Head Carol*. A version of it, dating from 1521, goes like this:

> Caput apri defero. Reddens laudes Domino,
> The boar's head in hand bear I,
> Bedecked with bays and rosemary,
> I pray you, my masters, be merry,
> Quot estis in convivio.
>
> The boar's head as I understand,
> Is the rarest dish in all this land,
> Which thus bedecked with a gay garland,
> Let us servire cantico.
> Our steward hath provided this,
> In honour of the King of bliss,
> Which on this day to be served is,
> In Reginensi atrio.

On New Year's Day the college Bursar goes round the hall and hands each Fellow and his guests a needle threaded with coloured silk. The colour of the thread is selected to correspond with the Faculty of the recipient. The Bursar says 'Take this and be thrifty', which means 'thrive' rather than 'save'. The recipient then fastens the needle in his lapel. The significance of the needle and thread lies in a pun on the founder's name (in translation): 'aiguille' – needle, and 'fil' – thread.

Queen's chapel, built in 1719 in the classical style, is open to the public for concerts, both at lunchtime and in the evening. The college library, built in 1696, has more than 100,000 volumes and is one of the most beautiful and important in the University; it was built by a former Provost, Timothy Halton. It owns four Shakespeare folios and a first edition of Milton's *Paradise Lost*. At one end is the painted figure of Queen Philippa. The hall (1715) has painted glass showing Philippa again, with Edward III, Edward IV and Charles I.

St Anne's College
Woodstock Road, Oxford OX2 6HS (0865   274800)

The College started with twenty-five female home students in 1879 as the Society of Oxford Home Students, became St Anne's Society in 1942, and a college ten years later.

The earliest college building is Hartland House, finished in 1938, and designed by Sir Giles Gilbert Scott. Up to this date, St Anne's ladies used hired rooms. Later buildings, the Wolfson Building (1964) and the Founder's Gatehouse (1966) have both won awards. Strangely enough, in view of the title 'Founder's Gatehouse', the College had no founder, but evolved from society to college over the years.

Old Girls of St Anne's include England's first lady barrister, Ivy Williams, and writers Elizabeth Jennings and Margaret Irwin. Today the College admits men as well as women.

St Catherine's College
Manor Road, Oxford OX1 3UJ (0865   271700)

'Catz', on the banks of the Cherwell, is one of Oxford's largest colleges. Its origins lie in a student society started in 1868 which developed into St Catherine's Society in 1930. The present college was built in 1960 to designs by the Danish architect Arne Jacobsen, and it is this Scandinavian uniformity which makes it unique. St Catherine's has a bell-tower eighty feet high

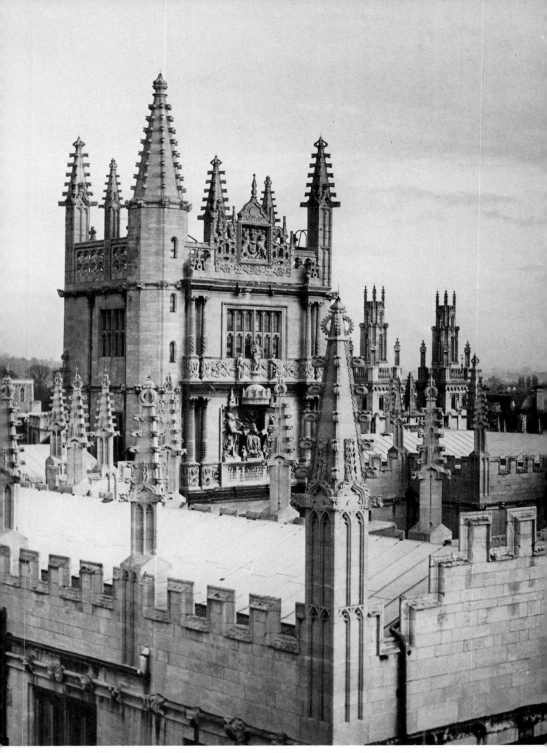

The Bodleian Library and the Tower of the Five Orders

The installation of the Chancellor of the University in the Sheldonian Theatre, then and now. *Above*: the installation of the Duke of Wellington in 1834; *below*: The installation of Mr Roy Jenkins (Lord Jenkins of Hillhead) in 1987

Viva in progress. A carving above the Examination Schools

Encaenia procession, 1904

The Radcliffe Camera and
Bodleian Library from the cupola
of the Sheldonian Theatre

An old map of Oxford. An
eighteenth-century print from a
sixteenth-century drawing

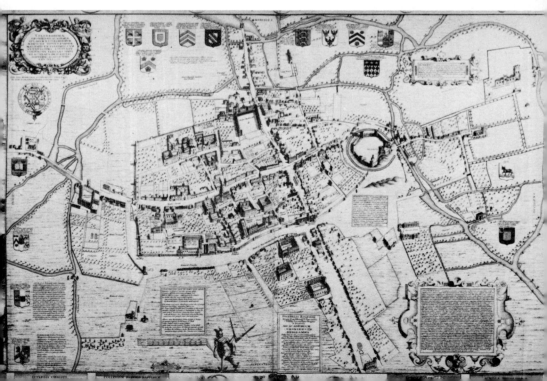

but no chapel, using instead the medieval church of St Cross.

St Edmund Hall
Queen's Lane, Oxford OX1 4AR (0865   279000)

'Teddy Hall' takes its name from St Edmund of Abingdon, Edmund Rich, who lectured in the infant University at the end of the twelfth century. It was founded in 1238, and is today the lone survivor of the dozens of medieval halls which have come and gone over the centuries. Full college status was granted in 1957 after the Hall had belonged to the Queen's College from 1557 until 1937; indeed, many people had assumed that it would finally be absorbed by its neighbour. Today St Edmund Hall is one of the larger colleges of the University.

The Front Quad, which is most attractive, with wistaria and a medieval well in the centre, was constructed over several centuries, from Tudor times until our own, all in harmony. Part of the east range is occupied by the chapel (1682) with Pre-Raphaelite glass by William Morris and Edward Burne-Jones. Nearby is the old library. Beyond the chapel is a very modern hall, the full name of which is the Wolfson dining hall. Like Lincoln, Teddy Hall has a disused parish church for its library (page 104). This library is open to readers day and night.

In the late 1980s, it was discovered that St Edmund Hall, along with Keble, had forgotten to alter its statutes to admit women, although it had accepted them since 1978.

The High Street extensions, completed in the 1970s, blend in exceptionally well with the rest of that historic street. They are named after White Hall, a medieval hall which once stood there, and are student accommodation.

St Hilda's College
Cowley Place, Oxford OX4 1DY (0865   276884)

St Hilda's was founded in 1893, as a hall, by Miss Dorothea Beale, Principal of Cheltenham Ladies' College from 1858 to 1906, in order that its ladies might have the chance to study in Oxford. It started with seven students, all but one of whom were from Cheltenham, and, to this day, a link remains between the two Colleges. The foundress gave St Hilda's an unusually good start by buying the Georgian Cowley House for £5,000. The building is now known as Old Hall.

The College's lovely grounds include woodland, and gardens which run down to the Cherwell, with plenty of scope for watching punts go by, and a view across to the playing-field of Magdalen College School.

St Hilda's has produced a Merton Professor of English Literature (1966–75) in Dame Helen Gardner. It offers some impressive bursaries provided by the Laura Ashley Foundation, and there are strong overseas connections at all levels.

The College shares a music society with Oriel and a joint choir with Christ Church, all in the musical tradition which produced the late Jacqueline du Prè, OBE, Honorary Fellow of St Hilda's, who was awarded an honorary Doctorate of Music at a special ceremony in 1984. Today, St Hilda's like Somerville remains single-sex.

St Hugh's College
St Margaret's Road, Oxford OX2 6LE (0865   274900)

Founded in 1886 by Miss Elizabeth Wordsworth, Principal of Lady Margaret Hall, St Hugh's was named after Bishop Hugh of Lincoln.

It started life in a private house in Norham Road, as a hall with four students under its first principal, Miss Charlotte Moberly. Both Miss Moberly and her friend Miss Jourdain, created a sensation when they claimed to have separately seen phantom visions of eighteenth-century Versailles while on a visit to Paris. So convinced were the ladies of what they had seen that Miss Moberly assembled the whole College to hear her account of what happened. Unfortunately, doubts were cast upon the veracity of both ladies, causing a considerable amount of bad feeling and indignation. The full story of what they saw may be read in Miss Jourdain's account, called *An Adventure*, and the story is included in many subsequent ghost books.

St Hugh's moved to new buildings on its present site in 1916, and became a military hospital on the outbreak of war in 1939, until 1945. Between those years students lodged in Holywell Manor, which belongs to Balliol. Although it contains no river, the garden of the College is nevertheless most attractive, being largely the result of imaginative planning by an Old Girl, the formidable Miss Annie Rogers. In 1873, Worcester College had offered an exhibition to a A.M.A.H. Rogers who had obtained the highest marks in the Oxford Senior Local school examinations. On learning that the 'A.' stood for Annie, however, the red-faced college immediately withdrew its offer!

ST JOHN'S COLLEGE

St Giles', Oxford OX1 3JP (0865   277300)

Title: The President and Scholar of St John Baptist College in the University of Oxford.

This, one of the University's most prestigious colleges in terms of both academic success and wealth, was founded in 1555. Its founder was Sir Thomas White, a merchant tailor who became Lord Mayor of London and named his new foundation after the patron saint of his craft. The site was formerly occupied by the Cistercian College of St Bernard, founded in 1437, only to be suppressed a century later by Henry VIII. In 1579, the parvis, or walled-in space, in front of St John's was purchased, and is now Oxford's only surviving example of this architectural feature.

Entry is by the gatehouse, above which sits St John himself, and into Front Quad. On its north side is the chapel, which dates from 1530 but has been much altered since then, principally by Blore in 1843. Here lie buried the founder, and Archbishop Juxon who attended Charles I on the scaffold and was bidden by that monarch to 'Remember'. Juxon was President of St John's, and, after his death, lay in state in the Divinity School. Another President was Archbishop Laud, a great benefactor of the college, who was beheaded in 1645. His body was first buried in the church of All Hallowes, Barking, before being brought to Oxford in 1663 to be reburied in his old college. In 1755, the heart of Richard Rawlinson, a great eccentric, was buried in the chapel, at the north end of the north aisle; the rest of Rawlinson lies in St Giles' church across the way. The hall (1500, enlarged in 1616) has been altered and restored over the years, but keeps its old collar-beam roof.

A central arch leads into Canterbury Quad, built mainly in the 1630s, and the library (1596–8) while the rest of the Quad also dates from the early seventeenth century. Archbishop Laud paid for the cloisters on each side, and for the statues of Charles I and Henrietta Maria, by Le Sueur, which cost £400 for the pair. The library contains about 90,000 works, among which are several letters by Jane Austen, and the only known complete copy of Caxton's illustrated edition of *The Canterbury Tales*.

St John's has modern quads too: the North, and the South, or Dolphin Quad. The unusual Sir Thomas White Building (1976) contains the Junior and Middle Common Rooms as well as study-bedrooms. Beyond Canterbury Quad, stretching to Parks Road, are the college gardens, laid out by 'Capability' Brown (see page 113).

St John's College was once known for its enthusiasm in celebrating Christmas, and this before the time of Dickens and Prince Albert. Revelry was widespread in Oxford in the early seventeenth century, as most students stayed on during the holiday period. At St John's is a manuscript, 'The Christmas Prince', which describes in detail the plays, the choosing of the Lord of Misrule from among the undergraduate body, the pageant, and the rest of the junketing. The college, like the Queen's, also held a Boar's Head Dinner. Today, the college drama group is called the St John's Mummers.

A certain early eighteenth-century bursar made himself unpopular by cutting down healthy trees in 1726. This provoked the following verse:

> Indulgent Nature to each kind bestows,
> A secret instinct to discern its foes,
> The goose, a silly bird, avoids the fox,
> Lambs fly from wolves, and sailors steer from rocks,
> A rogue the gallows as his fate forsees,
> And bears a like antipathy to trees!

ST PETER'S COLLEGE
New Inn Hall Street, Oxford, OX1 2DL (0865   278900)

The college was founded in 1929 as a memorial to Francis Chavasse, Bishop of Liverpool, who had been rector of Oxford's

St Peter-le-Bailey church from 1878 to 1900. Part of the site was that of New Inn Hall, which gave the street its present name, the old one being Seven Deadly Sins Lane! The Master's Lodgings, in Bulwarks Lane, were once the headquarters of the Oxford Canal Company, and the entrance to the college (1797) was part of the Company buildings. The library was once the rectory of St Peter's church, and the church itself is now the college chapel. It contains relics, mainly memorials, from the former medieval church of the same name, which stood near what is now Bonn Square. The east window (1964) has a coat of arms supported by a tortoise and a squirrel, and a large plaster cast taken from the tomb of Bishop Chavasse (1928) in Liverpool Cathedral.

SOMERVILLE COLLEGE
Woodstock Road, Oxford OX2 6HD (0865   270600)

Founded in 1879 as Somerville Hall, and named after Mary Somerville, the Scottish scientist and mathematician, Somerville became a college in 1894. It was undenominational, and, indeed, had no chapel at all until 1935. In addition to its twelve students, Somerville started off with a small menagerie of domestic animals, including a pony called, Nobby, and a bath chair in the depths of which Somervilleians could be conveyed to dinner parties without being gazed upon.

The original hall of residence, Walton House, was purchased from St John's College, which at first rented it to Somerville; later buildings include work by Sir Thomas Jackson, and by Champneys.

An interesting quotation from the College entry in the *Oxford University Undergraduate Prospectus* states that, 'many people have misconceptions about what a women's college is like. Some think it is a convent or an easy option. It is neither.', thus reminding us that Somerville, with St Hilda's, is still single-sex.

Former Somerville members include Dorothy L. Sayers, in whose novel *Gaudy Night*, the College forms an obvious background; Esther Rantzen of *That's Life!* fame; Shirley Williams, the first Social Democrat Party M.P. to be elected (in 1981); and two Prime Ministers, Mrs Indira Gandhi of India, and Britain's Mrs Thatcher. A Somerville Nobel Prizewinner for Chemistry (1964), Miss Dorothy Hodgkin, did not get her honorary Doctorate of Science until 1987, however, at a special inaugural ceremony for the new Chancellor of the University, Lord Jenkins of Hillhead.

TRINITY COLLEGE

Broad Street, Oxford OX1 3BH (0865   279900)

Title: The President, Fellows, and Scholars of the College of the Holy and Undivided Trinity in the University of Oxford, of the Foundation of Sir Thomas Pope, Knight.

Trinity was founded by Sir Thomas Pope, Privy Councillor to Henry VIII and close friend of Sir Thomas More, in 1555, the same year as St John's. Like its next-door neighbour and old enemy Balliol, Trinity might have seen something of the burning of the Oxford Martyrs only a few yards from its gates.

On the site of what was to become Trinity was Durham College, a Benedictine foundation of 1286, which was suppressed in 1544. Much of its fabric was incorporated into the new college's Durham Quad. In this quad are the chapel, library and hall. The chapel was built by a President of Trinity, Dr Bathurst, in 1691, and has much carved wood of a standard fine enough to be attributed to Grinling Gibbons, while the ceiling painting, by Pierre-Berchet, shows the Ascension. There are models of Sir Thomas Pope and his wife (1559).

Sir Christopher Wren, while still at work on the Sheldonian Theatre, opposite, designed the north side of Garden Quad in 1665, and it was completed in 1682.

The Trinity library is fifteenth-century, older than the college itself, with interesting glass showing the saints. Hall (1620) has unusual Swiss glass, made in the sixteenth century and donated to Trinity in 1877. There is the usual collection of college portraits.

Kettel Hall, in Broad Street, is a discreet distance away from the main buildings, and was designed for a President of that name in order that he might separate himself from his students. The custom of electing a Lady-Patroness, with a 'Poet Laureate' to sing her praises, was started by Samuel Johnson's friend,

Thomas Warton. Trinity allows All Souls men to row in its college Eight, because they are not in a position to form their own crew as All Souls is not a 'rowing' college.

UNIVERSITY COLLEGE

High Street, Oxford OX1 4BH (0865   276602)

Title: The Master and Fellows of the College of the Great Hall of the University, commonly called University College of Oxford.

In 1872 'Univ.' celebrated its millennium, still pretending to believe its claim to have been founded by Alfred the Great. At the celebrations, a small box was handed to the Master and was found to contain some burnt cakes, together with a letter saying that they had been dug up at Athelney, and a wish that 'King Alfred's scholars' would enjoy them!

The truth is that the college was founded in 1249 by William of Durham who had come to Oxford in the great exodus of British scholars from Paris in 1229. William left £206 14s 4d for the maintenance of a minimum of ten Masters of Arts, thus making University the third of the contenders for the title of Oxford's oldest college.

Architecturally, Univ. is a mélange of styles, from the sixteenth to the twentieth centuries, all on the site of Spicer's and Ludlow Halls. The fan-vaulting and coats of arms above the main entrance in High Street are well worth seeing, before turning right into the Shelley Memorial, which portrays the drowned poet (1822) executed in marble by Onslow Ford in 1894. It was intended to erect the memorial in the British Cemetery in Rome, but admission was refused.

The passage from Front Quad (1634–77) is the oldest part of the college, and leads into Radcliffe Quad (1716–19), named after the court physician, John Radcliffe, another University man. His statue, made in 1717 by Francis Bird at a cost of £70, stands above the gateway. A small gateway leads into the cobbled Logic Lane, running between the High and Merton Street, and forming part of Goodhart Quad (1962) which has mock-Tudor timber framing. The most modern Quad is Cecily's (1974); both these quads bear the names of a former Master and his wife.

Both chapel and hall are in Front Quad, the former with outstanding seventeenth-century glass and carving, the latter also seventeenth-century, with a hammerbeam roof from the Commonwealth period, and a remarkably fine organ.

At the beginning of this century, members of the college were wakened in the morning by the sound of the foot of the staircase being beaten with a heavy stick. Another custom which continued until 1864 took place each Easter Sunday, it was decided at a meeting, held that year, to discontinue it. After dinner the cook and his assistants would position themselves in the passage leading from the hall with a chopping-block decorated with flowers. As each Fellow left hall, he was presented with a blunted cleaver, and requested to 'chop the block'. Each Fellow was allowed to aim one blow, after which he handed back the cleaver to the cook, together with a gift of money. The origin of this custom is not known.

WADHAM COLLEGE

Parks Road, Oxford OX1 3PN (0865   277900)

Title: The Warden, Fellows, and Scholars of Wadham College in the University of Oxford.

The college was founded by a childless couple from Merifield, Somerset, Nicholas and Dorothy Wadham. As Nicholas died in 1609, Dorothy must be considered the real founder. The land, purchased by her in 1610, had been occupied by an Augustinian friary, and building began on Wadham in 1613. Wadham keeps a souvenir of its lady Founder: one of her shifts.

The original college buildings were so thoughtfully planned that little alteration has been necessary, apart from essential modernization and expansion. Dorothy had the sensible idea of positioning the Library above the kitchen, to prevent the books from getting damp.

When the present chapel was under construction, several skeletons, presumably those of friars, were found under a series of numbered stone slabs. It seems that they were re-interred, for these numbers can clearly be seen in the ante-chapel, forming a strange pattern with the swirls of light coming through the stained glass. Also in the ante-chapel is a seventeenth-century wooden clock-face, said to have been given by Wren, who was an undergraduate at Wadham. The chapel itself has a Jacobean oak communion table, which was donated to the college by Ilminster church, where the Wadhams are buried. The hall, next to the chapel but reached by stairs in Front Quad is flanked by statues of Dorothy and Nicholas, has fine carved wooden panelling and screen, a hammerbeam roof and a ghostly grey monk!

According to the original statutes, the Warden of Wadham was not allowed to marry, and it was not until 1806, when a special Act of Parliament was passed, that one did so.

Wadham's Beef Steak Club was a breakfasting society, founded in 1842, to promote 'good fellowship by periodical meetings at breakfast'. It had a tradition of electing three members for their athletic prowess and three for their intellectual merit. Firstly beefsteak and sausages were allowed, but kidneys were not admitted until the autumn of 1845, if sausages were not in season. Mutton chops however, were never allowed.

WORCESTER COLLEGE

Worcester Street, Oxford OX1 2HB (0865 278300)
Title: The Provost, Fellows, and Scholars of Worcester College in the University of Oxford.

For years Worcester College was known as 'Botany Bay' because of its remoteness from its fellow colleges; indeed, at one time it was even the home of a tribe of wallabies, but today the approach along Beaumont Street seems only a short walk from the centre.

Worcester was founded in 1714 under the terms of the will of Sir Thomas Cookes, who left £10,000 to build an 'ornamental pile'. Yet again, this is a college built on the site of a former monastic college, in this case the Benedictine Gloucester College, founded in 1283 by John Giffard. On the south side of Worcester's Main Quad are the medieval houses, or *camerae*, built by the various Benedictine monasteries which sent their monks to Oxford. Each *camera* had the arms of its community over the doorway. Gloucester College became Gloucester Hall in 1541, and was acquired by the Cookes Trustees in 1694.

Entry into Main Quad is by a Hawksmoor gateway (1736) from Worcester Street. The Quad has a cloister along its east side and a sunken lawn in its centre. The north side consists of the chapel, also by Hawksmoor, but rebuilt later in the eighteenth century; it has an altarpiece of the 'Entombment'. The chapel was built on the site of the old monastic church. Hall (1784) has an elaborate plaster ceiling by Wyatt and a portrait of Sir Thomas Cookes above the fireplace.

The library, on the east side of Front Quad, contains books which were once part of a collection owned by Charles I, as well as medieval manuscripts from Gloucester College. Off the south-east corner of Main Quad is the mainly fifteenth-century Pump Quad, another relic of Gloucester College.

Worcester's architecture, generally, is unusual in that it includes no important nineteenth- or early twentieth-century buildings. Its spacious grounds are particularly pleasant, and are the only ones to include a lake (see page 112).

THE POSTGRADUATE COLLEGES

Nuffield College
New Road OX1 1NF (0865   278500)
This was the first mixed college, named after and endowed by Lord Nuffield in 1937. It specializes in social studies, aiming to bring together academics and industrialists. Nuffield referred to it as 'that bloody Kremlin'.

St Antony's College
Woodstock Road, OX2 6JF (0865   59651)
Founded in 1948, by a French businessman, M. Antonin Besse, who was impressed with the Oxford graduates already in his employ. Attached to the college is the Nissan Corporation's Centre for Japanese Studies.

Linacre College
South Parks Road, OX1 3JA (0865 271650)
Founded in 1962 and named after the sixteenth-century founder of the Royal College of Physicians, Sir Thomas Linacre.

St Cross College
St Giles' OX1 3LZ (0865 278490)
This college was founded in 1965 and incorporates Pusey House, which is its theological department; otherwise research there is into any subject.

Wolfson College
Linton Road OX2 6UD (0865 274100)
Founded in 1966, another of the many benefactions of the Wolfson Foundation, with help from the Ford Foundation. It specializes in the natural sciences.

Green College
Woodstock Road, OX2 6HG (0865 274770)
Founded by, and named after, Dr and Mrs Cecil Green of Texas Instruments. It specializes in medical research.

Templeton College
Kennington, Oxford, OX1 5NY (0865 735422)
Admits a very small number of postgraduate students for advanced degrees in management studies. Although independent of the university, Templeton is affiliated to it.

PERMANENT PRIVATE HALLS

Greyfriars Hall
Iffley Road, Oxford OX4 1SB (0865 243694)
For members of the Franciscan order.

Regent's Park College
Pusey Street, Oxford OX1 2LB (0865   59887)
Founded for Baptist students.

Campion Hall
Brewer Street, Oxford OX1 1QS (0865   240861)
For members of the Society of Jesus.

St Benet's Hall
St Giles, Oxford OX1 3LN (0865   515006)
For members of the Benedictine order.

Mansfield College
Mansfield Road, Oxford OX1 3TF (0865 270999)
Founded for Nonconformists, but is today largely a lay college.

3 OTHER INSTITUTIONS

The Bodleian Library; The Divinity School; The Examination
Schools; The Oxford Union Society; The Radcliffe Buildings;
Rhodes Scholarships; The Sheldonian Theatre

THE BODLEIAN LIBRARY

The library takes its name from Sir Thomas Bodley, the
diplomat, who is buried in Merton College chapel. Although
sometimes credited with founding an Oxford University Library,
strictly speaking Bodley refounded it in 1602. The earlier
medieval library had been neglected and was finally dispersed in
the middle of the sixteenth century due to the political and
religious upheavals of the time, leaving the University without
its own, as opposed to college, library.

Besides replenishing the library, Bodley also endowed it, and,
in 1610, drew up an agreement with the Stationers' Company
(which then controlled copyright) to the effect that the
Bodleian should be entitled to one 'perfect copy' of every book
which they printed. This was the first library to be so entitled,
and therefore the Bodleian has the advantage of many early
treasures which others lack, particularly printed books.

Today the library is still entitled to this privilege, and has a
total of nearly five million volumes, with 973,000 maps, and
seventy-nine miles of shelving. Not only does it own books,
maps and manuscripts, but also paintings, furnishings and
mementoes of many famous men. The library's treasures include
the earliest manuscript of the *Chanson de Roland*, Fitzgerald's
own manuscript of *Omar Khayyám*, and several Shakespeare first
folios, to mention only a few. In the early 1980s, the Diocesan

records were transferred from the 'Bod.' to the County Record Office in the County Hall, New Road. Some of the colleges store their own collections of manuscripts in the Bodleian while others allow them to be read in the library when the need arises.

The oldest and most beautiful of the library buildings is Duke Humfrey's Library. This reading room was specially built to house the great collection of manuscripts given to the University by Humfrey, Duke of Gloucester, younger brother of King Henry V. At the time of the gift, the Divinity School was in the process of being constructed, and so the library was built above it, and finally finished in 1489. Unfortunately, only three of those first manuscripts have found their way back into the Bodleian's care. The two ends of Duke Humfrey's Library, which make this part of the top storey of the Bodleian into a capital 'I' shape, are Arts End (1610–12) and Selden End (1630s).

Old Schools Quad (1613–19) was adapted in 1789, and the first two floors used by the library. The names of the subjects once taught there may still be seen over the doorways.

The Radcliffe Camera by James Gibbs, completed in 1749, was originally a 'physic' library, but has been taken over as a reading room.

The central group in the Bodleian family of libraries consists of the Old and New Libraries, the Radcliffe Camera and the Clarendon Building. The Old Library contains the General Catalogue and the reference section, certain subjects such as English, Theology, Classics and History, as well as Western Manuscripts and early printed books in Duke Humfrey.

The New Bodleian, dating from the 1930s, with a foundation stone laid by Queen Mary, contains the bookstacks which extend underground, the Oriental and Maps sections, Music and modern manuscripts. In its roof extension is the 90,000-volume strong Indian Institute Library which covers works on all aspects of the sub-continent from ancient to modern times.

Other specialist libraries include the Hooke, a lending-library for undergraduate scientists; the Law Library in the St Cross Building complex; Rhodes House Library with its collections on the Commonwealth, the United States of America and Africa; and the Radcliffe Science Library, which houses the Bodleian's scientific department and is a neighbour of the University Museum. It started life in the Radcliffe Camera, then moved to the Museum. After having had several extensions added over the years, it now has more than twenty miles of shelf-space, holding about 800,000 volumes.

Admission to any part of the Bodleian and its satellite libraries is strictly by production of a reader's ticket. These are available to all members of the University and staff free of charge, to others by recommendation, while tickets may be issued on payment of a fee, for instance on a daily basis for specific research. The Library Admissions Office is in Schools Quad, under a doorway labelled 'Schola Musicae'; details may also be obtained from the secretary of the library. Before being issued with a ticket, all readers must 'recite and subscribe the statutory declaration', which includes, among other things, a promise not to kindle flames on the premises. During the period between Easter and the end of October, tours of the Divinity School and Duke Humfrey's Library are available.

THE DIVINITY SCHOOL

Oxford's Divinity School is one of the loveliest buildings in the city. It forms part of the Bodleian Library, but is easily missed by the unsuspecting visitor who is allowed in, free of charge.

Entrance is by way of Old Schools Quadrangle, behind the bronze statue of the Earl of Pembroke, and through a pair of heavy glass doors. This foyer, housing the Bodleian's shop, is the Proscholium, sometimes referred to as the Pig Market, from its function in the reign of Henry VIII.

The Divinity School itself was started in 1423, and financed by an appeal for funds. Contributors are still commemorated there by the display of their crests and initials on the magnificent ceiling bosses. The vaulting and decoration of this ceiling make the School well worth a visit.

Until recently a permanent display of some of the Bodleian's best-known treasures was mounted in the Divinity School, sometimes on a particular theme, but usually consisting of manuscripts, illuminated books, charters, letters, poems and first editions. Due to the threat of damage to these precious items, however, the display has been discontinued, but it is expected that the Exhibition Room next door in Schools Quad will be used to mount both permanent and temporary exhibitions, under more suitable storage conditions.

Meanwhile one has to be content with the architecture and history of the Divinity School itself, which, during the Seige of Oxford when it was the Royalist capital, was used as a storehouse and armoury. During the Commonwealth, the Commons met there to avoid the plague in London, and in 1663 the body of Archbishop Laud rested there before its re-interment in St John's College chapel. At the end of the seventeenth century the school was given a complete overhaul by Sir Christopher Wren, who constructed a new doorway in its north wall. Crowned with a canopy, it bears the initials 'CWA', for Christopher Wren, Architect. This doorway was built to give access to Wren's newly erected Sheldonian Theatre, which is adjoining. During degree ceremonies and Encaenia, the Divinity School is used for the registering of candidates and as a collection point for honorands awaiting admission to degrees.

THE EXAMINATION SCHOOLS
Corner of High Street and Merton Street

Before Easter 1882, when the present Examination Schools were first used, examinations were held in Old Schools Quadrangle, now part of the Bodleian Library. The only survivor to keep its original name, but not its function, is the Divinity School, although the names of the other subjects remain painted up over the various doors leading into the Bodleian.

The old schools were cramped and notoriously cold, as there was no form of heating allowed in order to safeguard the books. In winter, candidates had to resort to wearing top-coats and mufflers and bringing their own hot-water bottles.

The new schools were designed by T.G. (later Sir Thomas) Jackson, who also produced the organ case in the Sheldonian Theatre and Hertford College's 'Bridge of Sighs'. His inspiration was a stately home in Norfolk. The schools consist of a large entrance-hall or foyer, two large 'writing-rooms' which each hold 200 candidates, and a smaller one for 120. In addition, there are eleven smaller rooms, used for viva voce examinations and similar events, plus the examiners' rooms.

Today the Examination Schools are used not only for that express purpose, but also for lectures such as the annual Cyril Foster in Hilary Term, for the Freshers' Fair at the beginning of the academic year, and for conferences during the Long Vacation.

THE OXFORD UNION SOCIETY

Confusion often arises between the Oxford Union Society and the Oxford University Students' Union. The latter, as at most other universities, is a student association, which represents them on various committees, but the famous Oxford Union, as it is usually known, is in essence a debating society, membership of which is open to all members of the University, and which was founded in 1813.

Debates are normally arranged on Thursday or Friday evenings during term time, with attendance by guest speakers, many of whom are leading public figures, often statesmen or politicians.

The Union's premises incorporate a lending library, restaurant and bar, billiards room, and other amenities, and is the venue for film shows, discos and balls.

In 1933 the Union achieved worldwide and lasting notoriety when it voted that 'This House would in no circumstances fight for King and Country'. Before taking this claim too seriously, however, the reader should look at all the numerous war memorials in and around the college chapels. Apart from the Union itself and the OUSU, about 250 other societies exist, in varying states of patronage, to cater for every conceivable interest from Winnie the Pooh to tiddlywinks, and prospective members are wooed at the Freshers' Fair which is held in the Examination Schools at the beginning of Michaelmas term, and where each club and society has a stall of eager helpers ready to explain and enrol the new arrivals.

THE RADCLIFFE BUILDINGS

Dr John Radcliffe (1650–1714) was a Yorkshireman who became a member of both University and Lincoln Colleges and finally physician to William and Mary (of the former Radcliffe declared that he would not have his Majesty's two legs for his three Kingdoms) and, later, to Queen Anne. Under Radcliffe's will, trustees were appointed for the building of several Oxford institutions, and even the casual visitor is likely to come across at least one of these.

The most visible, the *Radcliffe Camera*, is now a reading-room of the Bodleian Library. Money was left in the will for the purpose of endowing a physic library, and the work was entrusted to James Gibbs, who beat Hawksmoor for the best design.

Gibbs had studied in Rome, and the Italianate influence is obvious in the domed rotunda, which stands alone in an open space specially cleared for the purpose. This is the area bordered by Brasenose and All Souls colleges, St Mary's church and the Bodleian Library, and known as Radcliffe Square. Below the lawn surrounding the Camera are two tiers of steel flooring, carrying movable bookcases. The Camera is not normally open to the general public.

Of more use to the citizens of Oxford is the *Radcliffe Infirmary*, in the Woodstock Road, which was opened in 1770. Next door, now in the grounds of Green College, is the Radcliffe Observatory, based on the Tower of the Winds in Athens (Keene and Wyatt, finished 1775).

Those persons who subscribed to the building costs of the infirmary were entitled to send cases for treatment there. There was, of course, no guarantee of a cure, as the *Jackson's Oxford Journal* for 2 February 1771 proves:

> At the last general meeting of the Governors of the Radcliffe Infirmary, it was resolved:
> 'That no Subscriber shall hereafter be obliged to bury any Patients they shall recommend to the said Infirmary, who may happen to die there, or be found incurable.'

In 1775, on 6 April, the infirmary appeared once more in the Journal:

Notice:
Any strong beer that is not fit for drinking will be an agreeable present for the use of the Surgeons.

There is a new, modern hospital, the *JRII*, to continue John Radcliffe's name, on a site in Headington, although the old infirmary continues to house some departments.

RHODES SCHOLARSHIPS

The system of awarding Rhodes Scholarships arouses a considerable amount of interest among visitors to Oxford from other English-speaking countries. Many of the honorands at Encaenia have spent part of their academic lives at Oxford, then returned home to embark on distinguished careers as statesmen and diplomats, scholars and scientists of world renown.

Well over 4,000 Rhodes Scholars have been through Oxford since the first ones arrived in 1903 under the terms of the will of Cecil Rhodes. He was an Oriel graduate, who, on settling in South Africa, made a huge fortune working for the De Beers diamond-mining Corporation. He also gave his name to the countries of Northern and Southern Rhodesia, now Zambia and Zimbabwe.

Rhodes died in 1902, and left £100,000 to his old college. The bulk of this was to go towards the upkeep of the fabric, but £10,000 was set aside so that the 'dignity and comfort' of Oriel's high table should be assured. An end product was the Rhodes Building (1909–11) and a statue of the benefactor perched on the High Street frontage.

Rhodes's will also specified that a number of scholarships be established, with the express purpose of bringing together the English-speaking peoples. Of these first scholarships, sixty were to go to the British Empire, and two to each American State. In a codicil added in 1901, he further specified that fifteen were to be awarded to German students. As he put it, 'a good understanding between England, Germany and the United

States of America, will secure the peace of the world, and educational relations form the strongest tie.' The Germans came until 1914, when their scholarships were suspended, and then revoked by Act of Parliament. In 1929 they were reinstated, only this time two each year, until they were cancelled once more in 1939.

Earlier Scholars were all men, but now women too are considered. There are about seventy successful applicants each year, chosen initially by a local committee in their own countries, their nominations being subject to the approval of the Rhodes Trustees. They are selected not only for their academic brilliance, but also for their qualities of leadership, their strong moral characters, and their sporting prowess. Rhodes was most insistent that they they should not be 'mere bookworms'. In addition, most already hold good degrees from their home universities.

Rhodes House

In 1929 Rhodes House, a highly individual building in South Parks Road, was opened. It serves both as a memorial to Cecil Rhodes, and as a headquarters for the Rhodes Trustees. It was designed by Sir Herbert Baker, and its rooms are named after some of Rhodes's friends, such as Jameson (of the 'Raid' fame) and Earl Grey, the tea connoisseur.

Rhodes House Library, named after Lord Rosebery, and now part of the Bodleian group, is devoted to works on the Empire, the Dominions and the Commonwealth, and the United States; in short, to the Scholars' own countries.

Over the door sails the Ship of State, its sails decorated with the English lion and the American eagle; also represented is the Zimbabwe bird, which gives its name to the new state, formerly Southern Rhodesia. A Greek inscription cut into the floor warns, 'Let no Smoke-bearing Person Enter'.

In 1983 a special reunion Congregation was held to celebrate the eightieth anniversary of the Rhodes Scholarships. After the awarding of several honorary degrees, degrees of all kinds were conferred on Scholars who had passed the relevant examinations, but, for some reason or another, had been unable to return to Oxford in order to be admitted.

THE SHELDONIAN THEATRE

Broad Street

The name, the shape and the function of the Sheldonian Theatre are all unusual. Firstly, it is not a theatre at all in the usual sense of the word, no plays ever having been put on there, but the ceremonial hall of the University where all ceremonies – degree, matriculation and Encaenia – all take place, as well as dozens of concerts, meetings of Congregation and Convocation, lectures and meetings.

The name and the shape derive from an ancient Roman theatre, the Theatre of Marcellus in Rome, but adapted for English needs. The name comes from the founder, Archbishop Gilbert Sheldon, who, in the early 1660s, decided that a secular building was needed in which to hold ceremonies and other non-ecclesiastical functions. Sheldon duly approached the young Christopher Wren, then only thirty-one years old and Professor of Astronomy, and asked him to submit plans and an estimate. Work started in 1664, continued until 1668, and the theatre was opened 'among great pompe and ceremony' as John Evelyn put it, on 9 July 1669.

Unusual features of the Sheldonian include the fact that the entire interior is made of wood, painted to look like marble. This was done partly to keep the cost down, but also to give good acoustics.

The ceiling painting represents an open sky, from which Truth is descending on the Arts and Sciences, as taught in the University in the mid-seventeenth century. Above the magnificent organ-case (T.G. Jackson, 1876) the black figure of Envy – generally known as Ignorance, Malice and Rapine being hidden by the organ-case – with snakes for hair, is being cast out by the combined efforts of Learning and Truth. The painting is in thirty-two separate panels, and was painted in Whitehall Palace, London, in 1668 by Charles II's serjeant-painter, Robert Streeter. It is on canvas stretched across boards, and was brought down to Oxford, by barge on the Thames.

However, it is the roof-timbers which are the theatre's major attraction for architects from all over the world. The area covered measures seventy feet by eighty feet, and is totally unsupported from below, as this would have ruined the effect of an open sky. Wren, assisted by his colleagues, devised a means of support, using trusses. Although the roof was replaced in 1800–1 and enormous Baltic cedars used, the original roof plan had to be adhered to in order to make the structure safe.

Likewise, Wren's original cupola has been replaced by a larger, bolder structure (Blore, 1838) but the view out over Oxford, from the famous towers and spires to the hills beyond, remains magnificent, once one has climbed the relatively comfortable 114 steps to get there.

The Sheldonian is open Monday to Saturday, mid-February to mid-November, 10 a.m. to 12.45 p.m. and 2 p.m. to 4.45 p.m., and from mid-November to mid-February, 2 p.m. to 3.45 p.m. Throughout the year the cupola closes fifteen minutes beforehand, both at lunchtime and in the afternoon. Admission charge includes ascent to the cupola. It should be noted that, due to the variety of functions held there, the Sheldonian Theatre is often closed for functions during the stated opening hours, and it would be advisable to check in advance, particularly on a Saturday.

4 THE LIVING UNIVERSITY

Applications and Admissions; Academic Dress; Matriculation; Examinations and Degrees; Officialdom; An Oxford Vocabulary

Oxford has always been a mass of contradictions, no less so today than at any other period in its history. Even the casual visitor is likely to experience some shattered illusions. To start with, not all the students, indeed, not even the majority, are upper-class 'Hooray Henries'; regional accents abound, not to mention foreign ones. Nowadays the University attempts to sell itself to state schools by means of a specially made video which seeks to dispel the *Brideshead Revisited* image which tended to put off many potential applicants. Secondly, members of the University do not go around all the time in medieval garb, flitting from tower to ivory tower, deep in contemplation. On the other hand, academic dress has not been discarded.

As regards the architecture, although Gothic, Classical, Neo-Gothick and heavy Victorian styles are only to be expected by any visitor, many are surprised to find the Bridge of Sighs, the Abbot's Kitchen from Glastonbury, and even ultra-modern egg-box designs. It is also worth noting that Oxford is the home of such modern equipment as the van der Graaf generator, especially as Cambridge is supposed to be the breeding-ground of Oxbridge scientists.

Perhaps what is most remarkable, however, is the average Oxonian's total unselfconsciousness while taking part in what, to the outsider, are somewhat weird and outdated ceremonies and rituals. Just watch the Encaenia procession wending its way,

full of Creweian Benefaction, through the city streets. Far from
being embarrassed or stage-struck by all the attention they
receive from foreign television crews and local people, the
participants act as if it is the most natural thing in the world.

This informality once extended as far as a certain
nonagenarian Chancellor, who had been placed for safety on a
chair in the Divinity School until the procession, with the
University Marshal at its head, should come to escort him across
the few yards to the Sheldonian Theatre. The Marshal, walking
so slowly that he was forced into a 'silly walk', as he afterwards
put it, realized the Chancellor's impatience when he heard,
quite distinctly from behind him, the growl 'Why doesn't he get
a bloody *move* on?'

APPLICATIONS AND ADMISSIONS

There are approximately 10,000 undergraduate and 4,000
postgraduate students in Oxford's thirty-five colleges and five
private halls at any one time. The question of who they are,
where they come from, and how they managed to get a place at
Oxford in the first place seems to fascinate visitors and tourists
from all over the world. An outline explanation is in order to
dispel some of the myths which have arisen over the years.

Firstly, anyone with suitable qualifications may apply,
regardless of religion, nationality and social class, entry being
strictly by merit; it is not possible under any circumstances to
pay to attend the University. British students come from state
schools (about forty-three per cent) from independent schools
(about fifty-four per cent) and from the various other types of
educational establishment, some of them overseas, which make
up the remainder; of these, nearly half are women. Thus the
traditional aristocratic undergraduate is nicely balanced today by
his state-educated counterpart; moreover, beneath the academic
dress one may glimpse all sorts of clothing: the universal jeans
and sweater, kilts, uniforms of the armed services, Buddhist
robes, and even, on one occasion, a cardinal's skull-cap peeping
out from under a mortar-board.

Application is made direct to the colleges of one's choice, not
to the University itself, and candidates are assessed for their

all-round ability and the contribution which they are likely to make to college life. Sporting hearties and 'mere bookworms', as Cecil Rhodes put it, are unlikely to do well if they cannot mix and adapt to the various activities which Oxford has to offer. All of the former men's colleges now accept women, although, rather surprisingly perhaps, neither St Hilda's nor Somerville accepts men.

ACADEMIC DRESS

A sight guaranteed to turn heads and start the cameras clicking is the appearance of members of the University proceeding through the streets of Oxford in academic dress. A relic of medieval formal attire modified by Puritan elements in order to eliminate certain undesirable 'Popish' aspects, the University uniform is sufficiently complex a subject for a book to have been devoted to it.

Although academic dress is not worn every day, usually only on certain set occasions such as sitting examinations or attending University ceremonies, it is still a common enough sight in modern Oxford. Gowns vary considerably according to both the status of the wearer and the occasion on which they are being worn (for instance, the dress of several doctorates comes in three versions: Full Dress, Convocation Habit and Undress); they range from the short, black cotton Commoner's gown, through the longer Bachelor's and Master's ones, with their differently coloured hoods, to the scarlet of the Doctors.

It is often said that it is possible to tell a graduate's subject by studying his dress, but this is not strictly so, as hoods and gowns denote the degree, not the subject, of the wearer, and, in addition, such varying degrees as Doctor of Literature and Doctor of Science, and Bachelor of Medicine and Bachelor of Civil Law, have identical academic dress.

The Vice-Chancellor wears the gown of his own degree with nothing to distinguish him, but the Proctors have special gowns with long, white fur hoods and blue velvet sleeves, while the Chancellor has a magnificent robe and train of black silk embroidered with gold, some of which came from Prince Charles's gown in which he was installed as Prince of Wales. In addition, the Chancellor wears a gold tassel on his mortar-board.

MATRICULATION

Although 'to matriculate' is often used in the sense of gaining the necessary qualifications to be admitted to a university course, at Oxford the matriculation ceremony is one at which new students are made full members of the University, and not merely members of their college.

A number of such ceremonies take place throughout the year, but the main one is in mid-October, at the end of the first week of Michaelmas Term. To be accurate, there are four ceremonies, one after the other, at which nearly 4,000 newcomers are matriculated, both post graduate and undergraduate.

The candidates assemble in the Sheldonian Theatre, college by college, and in academic dress, then the Dean of Degrees of the senior college present at that particular ceremony says to the Vice-Chancellor: 'Insignissime Vice-Cancellarie, praesentamus tibi hos nostros scholares ut referantur in Matriculam Universitatis.' To this, the VC, doffing his cap, replies with a corresponding Latin formula, then changes to English to give them a short welcoming speech.

After this the newcomers, who are then full members of the University, leave the building, and another thousand or so take their place and the ceremony starts all over again.

EXAMINATIONS AND DEGREES

Oxford undergraduates have two sets of examinations to contend with, the First Public Examination (or Prelims) normally taken towards the end of the first year, and the Second Public Examination, usually called Finals, which are sat during the student's last term at the University, after a course lasting three or sometimes four years. During the time that Finals are in progress, the area around the Examination Schools pulsates with hundreds of penguin-like figures dressed in 'sub fusc'. One story has it that a certain candidate, having read that an ancient statute allowed those sitting an exam to be served with ale to fortify them for the ordeal ahead, called for a pint to be brought him. The examiner complied with this request without question, then, quoting a second old statute, sent the candidate back to his college to fetch his sword!

Whether or not this story is true, what is certain that it is not a good idea to be around when 'Schools' come out, for fear of being swept along in the cork-popping, wine-swigging, back-slapping, foam-squirting masses. In spite of all this horseplay and bravado, the failure rate in Finals is astonishingly low, often in single figures; for instance only five failures out of 2,849 candidates in 1985.

All Oxford degrees are awarded by the University, and the same papers are taken by all students reading a particular option, regardless of their college. A new pass degree, the Bachelor of Fine Art, has recently been introduced, but the first degree is usually the BA Honours, which is to be awarded to successful scientists and engineers as well as to arts graduates, for there is no B.Sc. at Oxford at any level.

As at Cambridge and Dublin, Oxford requires no examination, no research, indeed no studying at all, for the Master of Arts. All one needs to do is to keep one's name on the college books for seven years after matriculation, pay college dues during this period, then, on payment of a further fee to the University, one is automatically entitled to supplicate for an MA. This is not, therefore, an academic qualification, but confers a sort of club membership of Convocation, and entitles one to vote for the Chancellor and the Professor of Poetry. It should be stressed that all other Bachelors', Masters', and Doctors' degrees entail a great deal of very hard work!

Degree Days

Unlike most universities, Oxford holds its degree ceremonies throughout the year. There are eighteen in all on nine Saturdays, one ceremony taking place in the morning and one in the afternoon, according to college. All ceremonies are held in the Sheldonian Theatre which was specially built for these events, and all are in Latin.

Strictly speaking, these are not graduation ceremonies, for there is no compulsion for a graduand to return at any specified time to collect a degree for they are not conferred by year, by college, or by subject. The dates of degree ceremonies are published in the *University Gazette* and those who are qualified and wish to attend a certain ceremony make application to their college to do so. Those who cannot may have their degrees conferred 'in absentia', while those who are not interested simply stay away. It is not permissible, however, to call oneself a Bachelor, Master, or Doctor of the University until one has actually been admitted to that degree, regardless of examination results.

At a degree ceremony, the Vice-Chancellor (not the Chancellor) presides, assisted by the two Proctors, and degrees are conferred in order, from the highest, the Doctorates, to the lowest, the Bachelor of Fine Art. Candidates are brought forward by their Deans of Degrees and are admitted by the VC, sometimes singly, sometimes in batches according to their status. Candidates for certain degrees, notably MAs, are gently tapped on the head with a New Testament while they kneel in front of him; they are not 'all banged on the head with a big book' as is so often stated! Another source of inaccuracy is the Proctors' Walk which takes place during the ceremony. It is often said that this would give any creditors an opportunity to pluck the Proctors' sleeves as they passed by, and thus object to a candidate's receiving his degree. This fallacy probably arose from the time when the Proctors used to collect votes from Masters and keep them in their 'tippets'; at no time would a tradesman, particularly one with such an end in mind, have been allowed near participants.

Once a graduand has been admitted to a degree, he or she goes out into the quadrangle, changes into the new gown appropriate to the degree he has just received and which has been brought from his college by a 'scout', and forms up again into a line to re-enter the Theatre to the loud applause of all the admiring friends and relatives there assembled.

Encaenia

Encaenia, which derives its name from the Greek for renewal, commemorates both the opening of the Sheldonian Theatre in July 1669, and the University's benefactors over the centuries; it is pronounced 'Enseenya'. Often referred to in old books as 'Commemoration', Encaenia takes place at the end of Trinity Term, on the last Wednesday in June, and it is the ceremony at which honorary degrees are conferred on famous people from all over the world and from all walks of life. In addition, it is a sort of going-away party and the highlight of the academic year. Having partaken of Lord Crewe's Benefaction, which is described in Chapter 2, a procession makes its way through the camera-lined streets, Chancellor and Proctors at its head, to the Divinity School where it sheds the honorands and proceeds into the Sheldonian Theatre on the stroke of noon. Inside, the scene defies description; it is a kaleidoscope of red, gold and black, classical, medieval and renaissance, but, at the same time, immediate and very real.

The National Anthem is sung to the accompaniment of the theatre's organ, and the Chancellor opens a Congregation. After the six or so honorary degrees have been publicly approved, the Bedels are dispatched to escort the honorands from the Divinity School. Each is introduced in turn, according to the precedence of the degrees which they are about to receive (strangely enough, there is never an honorary Doctorate of Medicine) and the Public Orator gives a Latin speech explaining the merits of each. Luckily, a bilingual programme is provided so that everyone present may follow the ceremony and thus appreciate both the honorands and the oratory.

With a welcoming speech and a handshake, the Chancellor presents the new doctor with a scroll. Honorands include such diverse personalities as John Evelyn, General Eisenhower, Prince Charles, Mrs Gandhi, Haydn, the Duke of Wellington, Margot Fonteyn, Rudyard Kipling, the Prince Regent, Andrès Segovia and Charlie Chaplin!

After the admission, the winners of certain University prizes recite extracts from their masterpieces; previous winners include

Oscar Wilde and Matthew Arnold, although gaining a prize has been said to mean the kiss of death for aspiring writers! Lastly, the Creweian Oration, a resumé of the year's appointments, retirements and bereavements, the gifts, endowments and purchases, the disappointments and triumphs, is delivered by either the Orator or the Professor of Poetry.

So Encaenia draws to a close and is terminated by the Chancellor dissolving the Congregation and being escorted from the theatre by the Bedels, followed by the Honorands, the Heads of House and the senior doctors. A formal luncheon party in All Souls College means another chance for the crowds in Radcliffe Square, the countless visitors and tourists, and even the faithful townspeople who have waited outside for the procession to re-emerge. For once, Town is extraordinarily proud of Gown!

OFFICIALDOM

The *Chancellorship* of Oxford University is largely an honorary position, the holder being a distinguished figure in public life, usually a statesman or member of the aristocracy. It is a life appointment, the result of an election by members of Convocation.

The Chancellor normally appears in his formal capacity only at Encaenia and other similar events such as visits by royalty or heads of state, but he may also be invited to come to the University as a guest or as a member of his own college, for he is likely to be an Oxford graduate, or at least an honorary Fellow of one of the colleges.

Former holders of the office include Robert Dudley, Earl of Leicester (1564), Archbishop Laud (1630), both Oliver and Richard Cromwell (1650 and 1657), the Earl of Clarendon (1660), Lord North (1772) and the Duke of Wellington (1834). The present Chancellor is Lord Jenkins of Hillhead who succeeded the Earl of Stockton (Mr Harold Macmillan) in 1987.

The *Vice-Chancellor* wields a considerable amount of power in University life. Not only is he a respected member of the University in his own right, he also confers degrees at all degree ceremonies, and may stand in for the Chancellor at Encaenia. In addition he sits *ex officio* on all university committees, and acts as spokesman and representative of the University.

Until 1969 it was the Chancellor's right to nominate the VC, but now he or she is elected every four years. Although there has never been a woman Vice-Chancellor to date, such a thing is perfectly permissible, and there has been a lady Pro-Vice-Chancellor. A maximum of six Pro-VCs are admitted at the same time as the VC himself, in early October. In theory any Oxford Master of Arts may hold the office of Vice-Chancellor but in practice it is usual for a Head of House to do so. A glance down the list of former Vice-Chancellors reveals some rather odd names, including Accepted (or Gracious) Frewin, President of Magdalen, who held office in 1628 and again in 1638.

Assisting the Chancellor and Vice-Chancellor are the *Proctors* (an office which has existed since 1267 and which features in practically every novel about Oxford and Cambridge) who are the equivalent of the prefects in any good, old-fashioned boys' school story.

There are two Proctors; they hold the position for a year, and are installed each March, along with their nominated deputies, the Pro-Proctors. Two colleges elect the Proctors according to a rota, and the Pro-Proctors come from the same two colleges as the Proctors themselves. There is a Junior and a Senior Proctor, the latter being the first to have taken an MA. Both take a very active part in Oxford life, sitting on most committees, regulating University clubs and societies, and figuring largely in degree ceremonies. Other duties include providing a counselling service, and standing at the head of the University police force.

Former Proctors include Thankful Owen of Lincoln College (1650) and one who, it is hoped, did not live up to his name, Savage Tyndall of All Souls College (1740).

The *University Marshal* is the head of the 'Proctors' Servants', a diplomatic term for the University police, the Constables of which are the world-famous Bulldogs. As his title suggests, the Marshal is responsible for organizing processions, supervising ceremonies, and checking that academic dress is being correctly worn. His own dress includes a very grand black velvet cape, while he wears a large silver badge on his arm, and carries an ebony wand tipped with silver. The whole outfit is topped with a Tudor-style black velvet bonnet.

He is assisted in his ceremonial responsibilities by the *Bedels* (stress on the second syllable) who normally number four, with an additional pair in attendance at honorary degree ceremonies. The Bedels are appointed by the Vice-Chancellor and the Proctors, and at least one is present at all official functions to escort the VC.

The Four Bedels represent the faculties of Divinity, Law, Medicine and Arts, in order of seniority, the three senior Bedels carrying gold staves while the Bedel of Arts bears a silver one.

Also present at Encaenia are the two *Cloakmen*, their titles reminding us of the days when gentlemen wore cloaks and needed someone to hold them during ceremonies when they were attired in their academic dress. The Cloakmen themselves actually wear cloaks which button up to the neck and reach down to the floor, for all the world like elderly Christ's Hospital schoolboys.

The office of *Public Orator* was first permanently established in 1564, with a stipend of twenty nobles (£6 13s 4d) annually, payable from the University Chest; this amount has increased somewhat since then.

The Orator, who must be a Classics don, is elected by Congregation from members of Convocation, and his duties include the presenting of candidates for honorary degrees, and the writing of a speech in Latin in praise of each one. He also composes official letters and addresses on behalf of the University, speeches to welcome royalty and other important visitors, and takes turns, with the Professor of Poetry, to deliver the Creweian Oration at Encaenia. Former Orators include the Metaphysical poet George Herbert (1620).

Apart from those Chairs founded by monarchs, various benefactors over the centuries have decided to endow a *professorship* at Oxford which has been named after them. Today, however, it is

BLACKWELL'S

B. H. BLACKWELL LTD.

BROAD STREET OXFORD ENGLAND OX1 3BQ

TELEPHONE: STD 0865 792792　　TELEX: 83118

ORIGINAL

INVOICE

PAGE　1

INVOICE No.
37911333

ACCOUNT No.
71617612 /
000

Please quote invoice No.
and Account No. on all
correspondence

DATE & TAX POINT
05/12/90

£

SENT TO

DR ROBERT P NEUMAN
635 EL TORO WAY
DAVIS
CALIFORNIA 95616
U S A

CHARGED TO

DR ROBERT P NEUMAN
635 EL TORO WAY
DAVIS
CALIFORNIA 95616
U S A

03/30

CUSTOMER REFERENCE

09/11/90

ANDREWS CHRIS — OXFORD: INTRODUCTION AND GUIDE PBK 15.82 £7.95
PAPERBACK

09/11/90 N

GOODHART DANIEL — OXBRIDGE REJECT SOCIETY PK PAPERBACK 7.94 £3.99
09/11/90 N

HARRIS MOLLIE — PRIVIES GALORE PAPERBACK 13.83 £6.95
09/11/90 N

THOMAS DAVID — PICK OF PUNCH(1990) [PICK OF PUNCH] 25.85 £12.99
09/11/90 N

YURDAN, MARILYN — OXFORD : TOWN AND GOWN 25.77 £12.95
POSTAGE AND HANDLING 10.29 £5.17

TOTAL 99.50 £50.00
US.$

PAYMENT CAN BE MADE IN U.S.DOLLARS TO OUR ACCOUNT
AS FOLLOWS THE BANKERS TRUST CO., P.O.BOX 1452,
CHURCH STREET STATION, NEW YORK, NEW YORK 10249,
U.S.A. A/C NO. 04800080

116 4936

VAT REG. No.: 194 2039 62   Giro Account 219100004 Bootle England   E. & O. E.

6

The Bulldog pub sign

Punts by Magdalen Bridge

Jesus College barge restored (since burnt out)

Celebration at Oriel College following the Bump Races of 1987

Torpids, 1989

The Proctors Walk, an ancient custom still observed when degrees are conferred

The Dining Hall, All Souls College

more likely to be large companies and foundations, such as Ford and Wolfson, who are the benefactors. Here are some of the older Chairs which are still extant in Oxford today.

Savilian Professorships of Geometry and Astronomy (Sir Henry Savile, 1619)

Sedleian Professorship of Natural Philosophy (Sir William Sedley, 1621)

White's Professorship of Moral Philosophy (Thomas White, 1621)

Camden Professorship of Ancient History (William Camden, 1622)

Heather Professorship of Music (William Heather, 1626)

Laudian Professorship of Arabic (Archbishop Laud, 1636)

Sherardian Professorship of Botany (William Sherard, 1734)

Vinerian Professorship of English Law (Charles Viner, 1758)

Rawlinson (now 'and Bosworth') Professorship of Anglo-Saxon (Richard Rawlinson, 1795, forty years after his death, as instructed)

Boden Professorship of Sanskrit (Joseph Boden, 1830)

Hope Professorship of Zoology (Entomology) (Frederick William Hope, 1861)

Slade Professorship of Fine Art (Felix Slade, 1869)

Nuffield Professorship of Anaesthetics, Clinical Medicine, Obstetrics and Gynaecology, Orthopaedic Surgery, and Surgery (William Morris, Lord Nuffield, 1936)

The office of *Professor of Poetry* dates back to 1709 under the terms of the will of a Henry Birkhead. Candidates for the post need not necessarily be members of the University, although they usually are. The successful candidate holds office for five years, having been elected by Convocation, the voting being done by ballot sheet and being fed into the University computer so that the results are ready in a matter of minutes. The Professor's duties include delivering one public lecture a term, acting as judge for certain University prizes, and delivering the Creweian Oration on alternate years.

Former Professors of Poetry are John Keble (1831), Matthew

Arnold (1857) and Francis Turner Palgrave (of *Golden Treasury* fame, 1885).

Heads of House is the term used for college heads in general, but one has to learn the correct appellation for the head of each individual college if wishing to speak of them separately. Most of the modern colleges have Principals, as do St Edmund Hall, Brasenose, Jesus, and Hertford Colleges. There are Wardens of Merton, New College, All Souls and Wadham, Masters of University, Balliol and Pembroke, Rectors of Exeter and Lincoln, Provosts of the Queen's, Oriel and Worcester, Presidents of Magdalen, Corpus Christi, St John's, Wolfson and Trinity, while the head of Christ Church is unique in being the Dean of a Chapter and also head of Oxford Cathedral.

Terrae Filius

The Terrae Filius ('son of the earth' in Latin) or University buffoon, was certainly a character throughout the centuries. Originally appointed by the Proctors to take part in the disputations at the Vesperiae (solemn disputations held on the eve of a candidate's acceptance as Master of Arts, an event which was also a time for horseplay, and ended up as something like the modern stag-night) and also at the Comita, the occasion for the actual granting of degrees.

The practice of appointing the Filius may have started about the time of the Reformation, and was certainly in full swing by Shakespeare's day, when he 'delighted his contemporaries with solemn fooling' as C.E. Mallet puts it in his book, *A History of the University of Oxford. Vol. II: the Sixteenth and Seventeenth Centuries*. This lighthearted debating was on 'fun' topics, in order to give candidates an opportunity of displaying their powers of rhetoric, rather than ability to learn things by heart.

The names of the Filii from 1591 to 1763 have come down to us, along with some fifteen of their speeches, the earliest being that delivered by Thomas Tomkins in 1607. In the seventeenth century, however, the position deteriorated, as first 'levity', then disorder, and finally 'lewdness', that favourite word of our Tudor and Stuart ancestors, took over from wit and mental agility. It became bad enough for Gilbert Sheldon to feel obliged to start the fund for the construction of a secular building so that St Mary the Virgin church should no longer be profaned by such indignities.

During his Vice-Chancellorship, between 1652 and 1657, John Owen, Dean of Christ Church, became so incensed with the Terrae Filius of his day that he actually laid hands on him himself, hauled from his rostrum, and had him sent off to the Bocardo Prison over the North Gate.

Owen's successor, John Conant, Rector of Exeter, tried unsuccessfully to suppress the position, once and for all, as 'scandalising decorous minds'. One of the tribe, Lancelot Addison, who was to become a Dean, and the father of the writer, Joseph, was obliged to go down on bended knee to implore forgiveness for the offence which he had caused. He well knew that expulsion was not unknown, for, far from being rough and ignorant persons who knew nothing better, the Terrae Filii were well-established members of the University.

Three examples of those who were expelled from their position were Hoskyns of New College, expelled in 1591 for being 'bitterly satyrical', Mr Masters, in 1632, but restored six years later, and Thomas Pittis of Trinity in 1658.

At the opening of the Sheldonian Theatre in 1659, John Evelyn called the Terrae Filius's efforts 'tedious, abusive, sarcastical, and rhapsodic'. This was Thomas Hayes of Brasenose, who went on to take his MD the same day. Evelyn complained to the Vice-Chancellor, and to several Heads of House, who were 'perfectly asham'd' about the whole performance as it was both personal and nasty.

By 1713 things were certainly no better, and the speech of that year was burned, before it could be delivered, by a Bedel at the command of Convocation. After this year the old 'Act', the occasion for conferring of degrees, which went on for several days and was accompanied by music feasting and entertainment, consisted of only a sermon and Encaenia, the giving of honorary degrees to distinguished persons. Terrae Filius was suppressed as a regular contributor.

In 1721 a publication entitled '*Terrae Filius, or the Secret History of the University of Oxford*', claiming to be by 'one of the family', appeared in fifty parts.

In 1733, however, the Act, accompanied by Terrae Filius, was revived for that year only. Handel came, and put the noses of local musicians and their supporters quite out of joint by charging entry fees for his newly written work, *Athalia*.

That year Terrae Filius's speech went from bad to worse. He started by calling the Bishop a 'mitred' hog, and querying his association with an eighteen-year-old wife. He then proceeded to vilify most of the colleges: Christ Church (always a popular target as an arrogant college) was slated for calling all other members of the University 'squils' and 'hodsmen', or snails, and had a 'courtier' for a Dean; 'Belial' men ate raw turnips; St John's men were 'Jacobite topers'; Exeter was governed by old women; members of All Souls were all body and no soul; Oriel men were all in debt; Magdalen dons loose livers; Lincoln College 'under the devil's inspection'; Mertonians 'Lollards'; those from Worcester practically incapable of reading prayers in English, leave alone Latin; while, it seems, Jesus College was 'verminous and smelled of toasted cheese'. Terrae Filius actually appeared, ready to deliver his speech, but, hardly surprisingly, he was 'not suffered' to make it.

In 1763, the seemingly irrepressible Filius turned up yet again, and this time included both Town and Gown in his attacks. He did, though, prove to be the last of his line, or nearly so.

Not quite, however, for 211 years later, in 1974, at the ceremony to welcome the two new fibre-glass Muses for the roof of the Clarendon Building, Terrae Filius was once again presiding, but this time in the guise of a Reverend gentleman, Graham Midgley of St Edmund Hall, who was a credit both to his college and the University!

AN OXFORD VOCABULARY

As in any other close community, particularly one as ancient as Oxford, a specialized vocabulary has evolved over the centuries. Some words and phrases are likely to be familiar to outsiders, such as 'quad', and 'dark blue', whilst some such as 'varsity' or 'grads' have become outdated. Others, however, may be known only to those who have contacts in Oxford or Cambridge, and it is useful to learn a little of the language in order to enjoy a visit to the full, and, indeed, to appreciate the unique flavour of Oxbridge life and tradition, as these terms are still used quite unselfconsciously in Oxford every day.

Battels: a member's account with his college for board, provisions and sundry expenses, bills being sent in at the end of each term.
Blue: an accolade awarded to someone representing Oxford against Cambridge (and vice versa) in any major sport; the person themselves.
BNC: Brasenose College.
Bumps: A peculiar form of inter-collegiate rowing during the weeks of 'Summer Eights' and 'Torpids'. College boats set off at regular intervals, trying to catch up with the stern of the boat in front. Successful bumpers are awarded a place in the next race, until eventually, by a kind of climbing-the-ladder process, one eight comes out on top and its college becomes Head of the River.
CCC: Corpus Christi College, in writing.
Ch. Ch.: Christ Church, in writing.
Come up: to start at Oxford, either initially or at the beginning of term.
Commoner: an undergraduate who has not gained a scholarship or exhibition to a college.
Commons: light meals or snacks available from the college buttery to be consumed in one's rooms, as opposed to being eaten in Hall.
Congregation: a body made up of all teaching or administrative staff of MA status or above.
Convocation: a body made up of all Oxford MAs anywhere in the world; membership entitles one to vote for the Chancellor and Professor of Poetry.
Deans: deans come in several guises: the Head of Christ Church; the welfare officer in a college, and the Deans of Degrees who present candidates at degree ceremonies.
Demiship: a type of scholarship at Magdalen.
Don: any senior member of the University engaged in teaching.
Eights Week: the five days (!) in late May which are devoted to

'bump' races on the Isis, the overall winner being the 'Head of the River'.

Encaenia: the honorary degree ceremony in late June.

Exhibition: a type of scholarship often given to students in actual need (as opposed to anyone clever enough to win one).

Gate: a verb meaning to confine to college for a set period, usually for staying out 'after hours'.

Gaudy: a celebratory feast or reunion of old members of a college.

Go down: to leave Oxford, either at the end of term or at the end of a course.

Greats: school of Literae Humaniores, Greek and Roman history, literature and philosophy.

Hall: rather than 'the' hall, not as glamorous full as empty.

Half-Blue: the equivalent of a Blue awarded for a minor sport.

Head of House: the blanket term for the head of a college, there being several different titles in use, depending on the college concerned..

Hebdomadal Council: often just 'Council', elected from Congregation and meeting weekly during term time.

Hilary Term: the spring term running from January to March.

The House: Christ Church, from its Latin name, Aedes Christi, or Christ's House.

Isis: the name for the River Thames as it flows through Oxford.

JCR, MCR, SCR: Junior, Middle and Senior Common Rooms.

Junior Member: one yet to become a member of Convocation.

LMH: Lady Margaret Hall.

Michaelmas Term: the autumn term running from October to December.

Modern Greats: Philosophy, Politics and Economics (also called PPE).

Oxbridge: relating to both Oxford and Cambridge.

Postmastership: type of scholarship at Merton College.

Read: one 'reads' a subject rather than studies it.

Rusticate: to send away from the University for a specific amount of time.

Schools: the Examination Schools, either as a building or as final exams.

Sconce: to challenge someone to down a large quantity of beer without pausing for breath, for committing some social indiscretion such as discussing women, politics or religion in hall. The winner of the bet pays the cost. A sconce may also take the form of a fine.

Scout: college servant responsible for the cleaning, tidying and general maintenance of a number of student rooms.

Send down: expel from the University for ever.

Sub fusc: a uniform of dark suit or skirt, with white shirt or blouse, white tie for men, black for women, with mortarboard or cap, worn with, or as, academic dress.

Torpids: bump races held near the end of February as preliminaries to Eights Week; sometimes called 'Toggers' in old novels.

Trinity Term: the summer term running from April to June.

Viva: (rhymes with 'driver') short for *viva voce*, an additional live performance by a student to ascertain class of degree; compulsory part of a doctorate.

5 CHURCHES AND CHAPELS

Carfax Church Tower; Christ Church Cathedral; St Mary
Magdalen; St Mary the Virgin; St Michael-at-the-North-Gate;
St Peter-in-the-East; College Chapels.

Some of Oxford's churches have fared better than others. As has
already been mentioned, All Saints', the former City church, an
eighteenth-century successor of a Norman one which was
destroyed when its spire crashed down onto it in 1699, is now
the library of Lincoln College; similarly, St Peter-in-the-East is
St Edmund Hall library. Others have had less useful ends. St
Paul's, in Walton Street, was declared redundant, then unsafe,
and, after being used as an arts centre, closed once more; its
future is still uncertain. Street's 'Phil and Jim' in the Woodstock
Road, also redundant, became a night-shelter for the homeless,
while St Martin's Carfax, Holy Trinity in St Ebbe's, and St
George's in George Street, were demolished.

The remainder of the older Oxford churches have, in the
main, been restored so drastically that, apart from the odd arch
or fittings, they are not easily distinguishable from Victorian
churches. In this category are St Ebbe's, near the back of
Westgate Shopping Centre, and St Thomas's, near the railway
station, important in the history of the Oxford Movement, with
its medieval stonework showing up among the nineteenth-
century brick streets. St Aldate's (otherwise known as St Old's
or even St Tole's), although much altered and restored, has five
remaining Norman arches, and a south aisle six centuries old
built by a fishmonger-parishioner who became Mayor of Oxford.

There is no such saint as St Aldate; presumably the name is derived from 'Old Gate'. The church was mentioned in the press in March 1765, when a patten-pincher was at large in the parish, and stole no less than five pairs of ladies' footwear during divine service.

St Cross, or Holywell Church as it is sometimes known, has a Norman chancel arch, a thirteenth-century tower with a good sundial on it; the church's fabric is mainly fifteenth- and nineteenth-century work. Inside are copies of old masters. The churchyard contains 'many distinguished brains now gone to dust' (John Betjeman).

The first entirely new church to be built in Oxford since the Reformation, St Clement's, in the Marston Road, replaces a medieval church which once stood where the roundabout at the Plain is now, at the end of Magdalen Bridge. Built in 1828 by public subscription near the Cherwell in pseudo-Norman style, St Clement's was immediately christened 'the Boiled Rabbit' by its critics.

The remaining ancient city churches and several in the immediate vicinity are worth a look inside provided that they are not locked, a practice which is unfortunately becoming all too common today.

CARFAX CHURCH TOWER

Until 1896 when it was demolished to make way for an ever-increasing amount of traffic to-ing and fro-ing over the cross-roads, St Martin's Church stood on Carfax. What we see today is the tower, the body of the vanished church having stood on what is now the pavement. Carfax has always been the principal meeting place of the city, under the clock whose quarter-boys strike their bells every fifteen minutes. The only other remnants of St Martin's are the gateway with its carving of the saint dividing up his cloak with a beggar, and the little churchyard beyond, with its wooden seats. Penniless Bench, also called the Butter Bench from the sale of dairy produce there, long the haunt of beggars and idlers, was removed in 1747 as being 'only a receptacle for idle people'.

St Martin's was once the City Church, the Town equivalent

of the University Church of St Mary the Virgin, where the citizens would gather in times of danger, celebration or disaster. When the church was closed, its status was transferred to All Saints' and ultimately to St Michael-at-the-North Gate.

The famous Carfax conduit, built in 1616 to bring piped water to the city from Hinksey, stood at the cross-roads until 1896, when it too was taken down and sent off to Nuneham Park.

At one time Carfax Tower was higher than it is today, but the townsfolk were compelled to remove the top layer for fear that they might throw stones down onto the gownsmen below. One may climb the tower during the spring and summer months; there is a small charge.

Christ Church Cathedral

Not only is the Cathedral the principal church of the Oxford diocese, it is also the college chapel of Christ Church, making it the focal point for both college and city.

This is England's smallest cathedral, late Norman, on the site of a Saxon nunnery, founded, legend has it, by no less a person than Frideswide, Oxford's patron saint. The earliest cathedral was burnt down in a revengeful attack on a horde of Danes who happened to have taken shelter in it. The thirteenth-century spire is one of the oldest in the country.

Entering by either Tom Quad or the cloister, one of the first items of note is the Faith, Hope and Charity window, just inside the south door. It was made in 1871 to a design by William Morris.

Moving down into the south transept, the visitor finds a series of monuments to Cavaliers who died during the Civil War, while the court was at Oxford and the King living in Christ Church. Among them, but in unmarked graves, are his three young Stuart cousins. Nearby is the tomb of Robert King, last Abbot of Osney and first Bishop of Oxford, who died in 1557. Above it, in a stained-glass window, are shown King himself with Osney Abbey behind him, an important record of this long-vanished medieval landmark.

At the end of this transept, in St Lucy's Chapel, is the Becket window, made in 1320, showing the murder of St Thomas à

Becket in 1170. Until recently the Saint was minus his head, which was destroyed by order of Henry VIII, a monarch who had little time for those who defied kings. The head was replaced at the time by the college authorities with a piece of plain glass, doing as little harm as possible, but Thomas now has a fine, new head.

The chief glory of the Cathedral is the splendid choir, with its beautiful vaulted roof, executed in 1500 by William Orchard and reminiscent of his earlier work in the Divinity School. Four statues, of Saints Luke, Mary Magdalene, Catherine and Peter, were saved from the hands of iconoclasts by their remote positions.

During his restoration in the 1870s, Gilbert Scott arranged the seating plan in strict order, depending on the status of the worshipper, ranging from Canons to visitors.

Along the eastern wall are more windows by Burne-Jones and William Morris, the most interesting being in memory of Alice's sister, Edith Liddell, which shows her as St Catherine.

Between the Lady Chapel and the Latin Chapel is the Shrine of St Frideswide (c.680–735) built in 1289, destroyed at the Reformation and then remade at the end of the last century. A slab in the floor marks the supposed site of Frideswide's burial, after her removal from the shrine in Tudor times. Nearby is a most unusual oak watching chamber (c.1500) from which a vigil was kept to make sure that no harm befell the shrine. Here too are the three tombs, all of them fourteenth-century, of Lady Montacute, granddaughter of Simon de Montfort, and her ten children, of Prior Alexander de Sutton, and of John de Nowers.

At the end of the Latin Chapel is the St Frideswide window (1858), again by Burne-Jones, and, in the north wall, three fourteenth-century windows. At the western end of the north aisle is a painted window (1631) by van Linge, showing Jonah sitting under a gourd tree, looking out over the city of Nineveh. Jonah is composed of traditional stained glass, not painted like the rest of the window.

South of the Cathedral is the chapter house, part of St Frideswide's Priory, which stood on the site until 1525, when it was incorporated into Wolsey's new, but short-lived, Cardinal

College. The chapter house dates from about 1225, and replaces a Norman one which was burnt down. Today it houses an exhibition of church silver and other treasures from the Oxford diocese, as well as serving as the college souvenir and gift shop, selling, among other things, records and cassettes of the Cathedral choir, and Alice memorabilia. Next door, in the Slype, an audio-visual film is shown during the tourist season.

GODSTOW NUNNERY

Through the village of Wolvercote at the northern end of Port Meadow, standing on the far bank of the Thames, are the ruins of Godstow Nunnery, of which nothing much survives apart from a walled enclosure and the shell of the early sixteenth-century chapel.

The nunnery was founded in 1133 as a community of Benedictine nuns, and in 1139 its large church was dedicated to Saints Mary and John the Baptist, in the presence of King Stephen and his queen.

Although there are few material remains at Godstow, it has a place in local folklore, and, it would seem, several ghosts. Legend has it that, in the words of Oxford's own historian Anthony à Wood:

> in the church of the nunnery of Godstow ... was buried Rosamund ...
> who died before her father, Lord Clifford. Rosamund ... was in the
> flower of her youth concubine to King Henry II and afterwards a nun
> here. Over whose grave was this written:
>   Hic jacet in tumba Rosa mundi non rosa munda.
>   Non redolet sed olet, quae redolere solet.
> which is summarised by Wood as. 'Here lyethe in grave Rose of the
> world, but not clene rose.'

Apparently Rosamund repented of being Henry's concubine, helped, perhaps, by threats from his queen, Eleanor, and ended her days at Godstow, having fled from him to seek refuge here. She was welcomed by the nuns as a sinner reclaimed. When she died in 1177 a costly tomb was built for her, and this seems to have become something of a shrine. Whatever the truth of the matter, the powerful Bishop Hugh of Lincoln, in whose huge diocese Oxford lay until the Reformation, was so disgusted when he visited the nunnery in 1191 that a concubine should be resting in a rich shrine, that he ordered Rosamund's immediate eviction. Her bones were placed in a perfumed leather bag and re-interred in a stone coffin in the nunnery church.

Upon its dissolution in 1539, the nunnery became a private house, lived in by the King's physician, Dr Owen. It was fortified during the Civil War by the Royalist David Walter, whose monument is in Wolvercote church, only to be damaged by fire in 1645, and then easily destroyed by Fairfax the following year.

In *Jackson's Oxford Journal* of 21 January 1764, we read of further damage:

> The same Hurricane blew down the famous Ruin at Godstowe, about two miles above this City, which [i.e. the ruin] not only gratified the Curiosity of the Antiquarians as the only venerable Remain of the Monastic Church of Godstowe, but also furnished a most pleasing Object in that beautiul Landscape, as it recalled to our Minds the Memory of Fair Rosamund who was imprisoned here under the Displeasure of Queen Eleanor and afterwards buried in a private Chapel belonging to the Convent.

IFFLEY CHURCH

St Mary the Virgin, Iffley, was built by a member of the Norman family of St Remy in 1170, on the site of an earlier, Saxon, foundation. This Norman building had chancel, tower and nave, plus, it is believed, an apse to the east of what is the choir today.

Between the twelfth and the sixteenth centuries there was continual modernization; fortunately that carried out in our own time has been equally sympathetic, so that what we see today is one of the foremost Norman churches in England.

The three ornate Norman doorways command attention, the southern one in particular being of interest, with its symbols of good and evil; among the latter is shown Henry II! The fact that the carving is incomplete leads the experts to think that it was done in situ. The blocked-up arch could be either a priest's door, leading into an apse, or, more interestingly, a window giving a view of the altar and used by Annora, a thirteenth-century anchoress who lived nearby. Both this arch and a little window in the east gable may be Saxon. On the grass outside the west door is what appears to be a font, of unknown history.

Inside, on the north wall of the sanctuary, is a circular Agnus Dei, believed to be the head of the churchyard cross. Four of the original twelve consecration crosses remain, some, unfortunately, obscured.

The black stone font, which has three spiral columns and an odd, plain one, is large enough for a baby to be completely immersed.

The whole of the west window, including the surround, was put in in 1858, to replace a fifteenth-century one which had, in its turn, ousted the original Eye of God window. Glass fragments dating from the Middle Ages show the arms of John de la Pole, Duke of Suffolk. The modern font (1907) is by Ninian Comper.

ST MARY MAGDALEN

Magdalen Street

Unlike that of the college, the name of the church is pronounced as it is spelled, but it is often referred to as 'St Mary Mag's'. It is of Norman foundation, on a Saxon site, but the oldest parts of the existing church are thirteenth-century, the Norman chancel arch having been destroyed in 1841.

Unusually square in shape, the church is made up of chancel, nave and aisles. The northern Martyrs' aisle (1841) is to the memory of Ridley, Latimer and Cranmer, and financed by £8,000 left over after the Martyrs' memorial next door was paid for. The aisle, which is by Scott, is important architecturally, as it is the first piece of neo-Gothic to appear in Oxford. An older north aisle was added, or perhaps repaired, by Devorguilla de Balliol, as a temporary chapel for her new college.

The interior of St Mary's has more statues and candles than is usual in an Anglican church and is traditionally 'high church', with holy water stoups, Stations of the Cross and a statue of the Virgin Mary which wears a mantilla across its face during Lent.

There is one chest nearly seven centuries old, another

from the late seventeenth century, and an intricately carved font from the fourteenth. In the east window is the church's patron saint, and in others scenes showing saints associated with both the church and the city.

ST MARY THE VIRGIN

High Street

St Mary's church was mentioned in 'Domesday Book', and the present edifice which goes back to the late thirteenth century stands on the site of a Saxon building. Most of the existing fabric, however, is late fifteenth-century. Today's St Mary's stands proudly, its spire reaching nearly 200 feet into the Oxford skyline, its tower offering a view out over the dreaming spires all around. In August 1795 the spire was struck by lightning which perforated the clock, badly discolouring the figure XII.

The church is the venue for the University Sermons, preached every Sunday in term and attended by the Vice-Chancellor and the attendant Bedels. Until the opening of the Sheldonian Theatre in 1669, it was also the setting for all the University ceremonies. Adjoining its north-east corner, and now an integral part of it, is the early fourteenth-century Congregation House, the University's first building, as opposed to one belonging to a college. In 1320 a library room, the ancestor of the Bodleian and still used for functions, was added on top of Congregation House.

It was in St Mary's that John Wycliffe denounced the religious abuses of his day, and here Cranmer, Latimer and Ridley were summoned to appear to answer for their religious convictions. The marks of the platforming on which they stood while being examined by the commission of enquiry may be seen on the pillars to this day.

The oldest monument in St Mary's is the altar tomb of the founder of Oriel College, Adam de Brome, Almoner to Edward II. De Brome was Rector of St Mary's, and a much later incumbent was John Henry Newman, who later went over to Rome.

On a marble slab set into the floor not far from the sanctuary steps one reads that 'in a vault of brick, at the upper end of the quire of this church' lie the mortal remains of Amy Robsart. The unfortunate Amy was wife to Lord Robert Dudley, afterwards Earl of Leicester, and Chancellor of the University.

To the north of the church is its bookshop, where tickets to climb the tower may be bought.

St Michael-at-the-North Gate
Cornmarket Street

Now the City Church of Oxford, St Michael's is the oldest building in Oxford, because of its eleventh-century tower. It is possibly pre-Conquest, and definitely of Saxon, as opposed to Norman, workmanship. The North Gate, from which the church takes its name, was pulled down in 1771/2 under the terms of the Oxford Paving and Lighting Act.

The main part of St Michael's is medieval, and it owns the oldest stained glass in Oxford, from the thirteenth century. From the turn of the fifteenth comes the lily window, showing Christ rising from the heart of a lily flower.

The fourteenth-century font, which was brought from St Martin's, Carfax, when it was pulled down, must have been seen by Shakespeare when he stood as sponsor to the son of the landlord of 'The Crown' inn in Cornmarket, in 1606. Rumour has it that the poet was himself the lad's father. The fifteenth-century pulpit was used by John Wesley in 1726, when he preached the Michaelmas sermon from it as his first duty as newly elected Fellow of Lincoln College.

The Saxon tower has recently been adapted to house the church's library and treasury, with displays of plate, pictures and other valuables connected with the history of the church, including an eleventh-century fertility symbol known as a *sheela-na-gig*, and the door of the cell where the Oxford Martyrs were imprisoned in the Bocardo, above the North Gate. Further up are the belfries and clock-room, and, lastly, the roof and a view out over the city centre. In all, there are ninety-seven steps on several levels.

On Ascension Day, St Michael's continues the centuries-old

practice of beating the bounds, or parish boundaries. Those interested in the subject of parish boundaries and their markers, should go to Marks and Spencer's store in Queen Street, where not only is there a metal plaque set into the floor, but also a stone, in a glass case, which shows the parishes whose boundaries meet at this spot.

St Peter-in-the-East

Queen's Lane
The entrance to St Peter's is through St Edmund Hall. Now that the church is the college library, visitors are no longer admitted into the main body. The north chapel is thought to be that Lady Chapel which St Edmund of Abingdon founded, and paid for with money received from his lectures. The nave, chancel and remains of a round font are all Norman, as in the crypt, which dates from about 1130. St Peter-in-the-East was once the mother church for St Peter's, Wolvercote, a good three miles away. Visitors are allowed into the crypt by obtaining the key from the college lodge.

College Chapels

College chapels are normally open to the public both during college opening times and for Evensong in term-time. Like the colleges themselves, the chapels vary considerably, some being stately and elegant, some warm and welcoming, others bare and draughty. An outline of the chapel has been given under the description of each college in Chapter 2, but, apart from Christ Church, two other colleges have outstanding chapels.

Merton Chapel

Until the end of the last century, Merton chapel was also the parish church of St John the Baptist, with its own parish registers and records. The oldest part of the fabric is seven centuries old, the youngest 550 years.

Merton's lovely bell-tower, although nowhere near as tall as Magdalen's, is just as attractive, with little turrets and pinnacles bidding a welcome as one cuts through between Merton Street and Christ Church Meadow. The ante-chapel is large, bigger than some of the smaller chapels, and lined with monuments and memorial brasses. The most notable of the monuments are those to Sir Thomas Bodley, who is shown as a bearded bust, surrounded, as in life, by books, and to Sir Henry Savile. The strangest is, perhaps, to someone who was born, lived and died on Merton property, the seventeenth-century antiquarian and historian, Anthony à Wood, who, as we read in his *Life and Times*, chose this very spot as his final resting place, well before his death.

The collection of brasses is a good one, especially in the field of ecclesiatical specimens, of which the college has the oldest in Oxford, that of Richard de Hakebourne, who died in 1310.

Standing on the floor, near to Wood's wall-monument, is an outsize green marble font, or vase, given to the college by a Czar of Russia.

Inside the chapel proper is some of the oldest and loveliest glass in all Oxford, a few pieces as early as the thirteenth century together with much from the later Middle Ages, all rare survivors from what was considered an idolatrous age. Some of the glass, given in about 1300 by Henricus de Malmsfield, has no less than twenty-four little portraits of the donor in it!

New College Chapel

There is much in the chapel that the founder, William of Wykeham, would recognize, including, of course, his own crozier and portrait. The oak roof has angels supported on corbels made from crowned and mitred heads. The stalls, heavily carved, have fourteenth-century work, well restored in the last century. Of sixty-two misereres, thirty-eight are original; on view to those who know just where to look are Jack and the Beanstalk, a doctor giving a lecture, demons and monsters. The large organ has more than 3,000 pipes, and the chapel is sometimes used for concerts and recitals.

The chief feature of New College chapel is its Te Deum reredos, which fills the entire east wall behind the altar. About fifty figures under canopies appear on it, rising upwards in tiers towards Christ in Glory. There is plenty of fourteenth-century glass in the north and south windows. The ante-chapel, too, has glass from that century, plus a Nativity by Reynolds in its west window, with the artist as a shepherd on the left. Still in the ante-chapel, the lover of medieval brasses will find one of the best galleries available here, gathered together and roped off for safety. There are many monuments all round the walls, including a war memorial from the Great War. This caused a great deal of controversy at the time as it included the names of New College members who had gone home to Germany to fight for their country. By the time that World War II monuments appeared, however, this practice caused no comment.

Under the west window of the ante-chapel is Epstein's 'Lazarus' bursting forth from his winding-sheet. Lazarus is one of the college favourites, and his absence is remarked on and accounted for whenever he is on loan at exhibitions.

To the west of the chapel is the cloister, which dates from the early days of the college, in the first year of the fifteenth century (i.e. 1400). It is lined with plaques and memorials to centuries of College members, both famous and obscure, and every so often along its length one comes across an enormous statue of a forgotten ecclesiastic personage, eyeless and battered now, poor soul.

A report in *Jackson's Oxford Journal* for 14 October 1778, shows the dangers of combining high fashion with visits to medieval chapels:

Last Tuesday evening as the Congregation at New College Chapel were quitting the service, a Lady's head, in the present fashion, took fire by coming in contact with one of the lights, the composition of this paraphernalia being comprised as usual of very combustible matter, the conflagration seemed very alarming, but a lady, having the Presence of Mind to push the whole Pile at once, the Flames were fortunately

extinguished without communicating to the Heads of any other of the
Ladies.

So this sudden alarm, which seemed pregnant with most fatal
Consequence, ended in Jocularity and was productive of many
Witticisms at the unfortunate Lady's expence.

Chapel Treasures

Those interested in what the various colleges have to offer in the
way of furnishings may find the following list useful; these are
outstanding examples, but most colleges have something to
show the art historian.

Window Glass
All Souls; portraits of saints and monarchs. *Balliol*: among the
finest fifteenth- and sixteenth-century examples. *Lincoln*:
seventeenth-century Biblical. *Queen's*: seventeenth-century by
van Linge. *St Edmund Hall*: Morris and Burne-Jones designs.
University: seventeenth-century, van Linge. *Wadham*: finest
seventeenth-century examples in Oxford.

Memorials
All Souls: monumental brasses. *Balliol*: brass plates to many
University Chancellors. *Magdalen*: brasses, mainly fifteenth- and
sixteenth-century. *New College*: brasses. *Queen's*: brasses.

Carving
All Souls: outstanding reredos, damaged at Reformation,
plastered over at Restoration, and restored by Scott, with about
135 statues. *Lincoln*: woodcarving in the Hall. *St Edmund Hall*:
seventeenth-century woodcarving. *Trinity*: Grinling Gibbons

woodcarving. *Wadham*: seventeenth century wooden box-pews, pulpit and stalls.

Benches and Stalls
All Souls: Lincoln, Magdalen; Trinity.

6 PARKS AND GARDENS, MEADOWS AND RIVERS

The Botanic Garden; Christ Church; Balliol College; Worcester College; St Edmund Hall; The Queen's College; St John's College; New College; Magdalen College; The University Parks; Christ Church Meadow; Angel and Greyhound Meadow; On the River at Oxford

Most Oxford colleges have fine gardens, whose origins lie in the medieval kitchen garden. At this period, one in Lincoln was actually known as the 'cooke's' garden. It was not until Tudor times that gardens were generally landscaped and formalized.

Today there are hidden or locked Fellows' gardens for senior members, tiny ones, like the Nun's Garden at Queen's, lovely riverside ones as at St Hilda's, which also has a fritillary meadow paid for by a peppercorn rent, shrubberies at Wadham, the sprawling, grassy areas of Trinity and beautifully kept lawns everywhere. One might add those at St Catherine's, Danish-designed like everything else in the college; Exeter's chestnut tree which stretches across Brasenose Lane (when it touches that college, Exeter is said to be about to beat Brasenose on the river); and last, but certainly not least, the herbaceous haunts of the Corpus Tortoise, a large reptile named Sheba who is not necessarily resident in the college, but who is owned by the Junior Common Room and is an honorary member.

On the damp but romantic evenings of Trinity Term, college drama societies offer such diverse productions as *Winnie the Pooh* and *Romeo and Juliet*, *Antigone* and *Alice through the Looking*

Glass. These are helped along, in the true Oxford tradition, by helpings of wine and strawberries.

Certain Oxford gardens, however, deserve special mention, as they are outstanding either for their size, their interest, or their beauty. In addition, many fine public parks and meadows of considerable size and antiquity come within the city boundary.

THE BOTANIC GARDEN

At the bottom of the High Street, opposite Magdalen College and between the Cherwell and Christ Church Meadow, is the oldest botanic garden in England.

It was laid out on the site of the old Jewish cemetery, abandoned when the Jews were expelled from the country in 1290, and established as a physic garden by the Earl of Danby in 1621. The entrance gate is named after the Earl, and has statues of both him and Charles II, clad somewhat incongruously in Roman costume. The garden's original function was to grow herbs for use in medicine, but it quickly became a centre of propagation for species brought back from the New World.

Mentioned in the diaries of both Pepys and Evelyn, the garden is laid out in much the same fashion as they would have seen it, and is still surrounded by the original wall, and so gives us some idea of how a Tudor or Stuart college garden would have appeared. Owing to the fact that one of its chief benefactors was Sir Joseph Banks, founder of the Royal Gardens at Kew, it could be said to be in one sense an ancestor of Kew Gardens.

By 1648, some 1,600 species were growing there, and in 1669 the first Professor of Botany was appointed.

Today, apart from being a very pleasant spot in which to spend a summer afternoon, and a mecca for garden-lovers, the Botanic Garden is an important centre for more serious studies, such as the economic factors involved in plant cultivation and their importance in the Third World.

A guidebook is on sale at the office; the greenhouses are open each afternoon between 2 and 4 p.m.

The Rose or Penicillin Garden, between the High Street and the entrance to the main garden, commemorates the development of penicillin in Oxford by Florey, after its discovery by Fleming.

CHRIST CHURCH

The college has a 'medieval' garden in what was once the cloister garth. It was designed by Mavis Batey, wife of one of the senior members, and, during its planning in 1985, Saxon remains were discovered. These confirmed many of the suppositions which had already been made concerning the origins of St Frideswide's Priory on the site, and, indeed, the legend of the saint herself. In 1518 Catherine of Aragon, the first queen of Henry VIII, came on a pilgrimage to Frideswide's shrine, accompanied by Cardinal Wolsey. The college pomegranate tree, the symbol of Catherine's homeland, commemorates this royal visit.

Christ Church also has a War Memorial Garden, laid out in 1925 and reached from St Aldate's through wrought-iron gates. Between the gates, set into the pavement, is a metal sword, with the inscription 'My sword I give to him that shall succeed me in my pilgrimage'. The quotation is from Bunyan's *Pilgrim's Progress*, the sword representing that of Mr Valiant-for-Truth. The gardens commemorate all Oxford men, whether from the University or the city, who lost their lives in the Great War.

BALLIOL COLLEGE

Probably the most attractive part of this college which is renowned more for its brains than its beauty, Balliol Fellows' Garden contains the so-called 'tomb' of Devorguilla, co-founder of the college with her lord, John de Balliol. In reality it is a collection of stones brought to the garden from an ancient entrance, demolished in the 1860s. The lady was buried at Sweetheart Abbey, on the Scottish Borders.

Balliol has an elderly mulberry tree which just could be one of those planted in response to James I's demands for the country to grow mulberry to feed a silkworm population, and so encourage sericulture. Unfortunately, this tree, like its relation at Merton in the Warden's Garden, bears black fruit, while only the white variety is acceptable to silkworms.

WORCESTER COLLEGE

No-one looking at Worcester from the outside would suspect that its grounds include a lake around which it is possible to stroll, and get right away from the traffic at the college's front door and the railway to its rear.

Under the Vice-Provost's garden is a tunnel, for all the world like the one along which the White Rabbit scurried, clutching his watch. It is probably the prototype of the tunnel which Lewis Carroll included in his book.

ST EDMUND HALL

The medieval well which sits in the middle of the quad was rediscovered in 1927 and given a new well-head and a Latin inscription which translates: 'Therefore with joy shall ye draw water out of the wells of salvation.'

Teddy Hall has a unique garden in the churchyard of the former parish church of St Peter-in-the-East. This beautifully tended spot is well provided with seats and litter bins and is an ideal place in which to eat one's lunch on a fine day. One of the seats bears the legend 'AM e^2/c, D.G.', thus rendering thanks to God for a discovery in quantum mechanics!

THE QUEEN'S COLLEGE

Here is one of the smallest, least-known and yet most appealing of all Oxford gardens. Known as the Nun's Garden, it would seem to have no connection whatsoever with religious ladies, but to have been named for a now forgotten Mr Nunn who once enjoyed relaxing there. It is reached through the second gate to the left at the end of a long, stony path lined with toad-flax.

In the same college is the little Drawda Garden, which derives its title from one William of Drogheda, a thirteenth-century Irish canon who gave his name to an adjacent hall. Among the roses is an eagle, for the college's founder was Robert de Eglesfield.

The Queen's College's only surviving specimen of medieval stonework is another play on words, this time a carved rebus on the name Robert Langton of Winchester. This incorporates a wine barrel, or 'wine-tun', meaning Wintonensis, or 'of

Winchester'. This carving may be found in the Fellows' Garden, in the corner furthest from the entry.

ST JOHN'S COLLEGE

The garden of St John's lies beyond Canterbury Quad, deep in the heart of the college. Immediately to its left is the rock garden which includes almost 700 species, most of which are alpines.

The main garden was laid out by 'Capability' Brown, and is among the finest and largest in Oxford, as well as the most colourful, for it has something to offer all the year round. In the summer there are wonderful rhododendrons, most unusual for Oxford, where the soil has too high a lime content for these plants to thrive. The secret at St John's has been to plant them in enormous holes filled with peat, an idea which has also worked successfully with the lilies and camellias. In the autumn the changing colours of the leaves are well worth a visit.

NEW COLLEGE

This is possibly the most interesting of the college gardens. Like the rest of New College, it is on the supposed site of an old plague-pit. The mound in the centre of the garden, however, was never used for burials, being merely a focal point; it was first mentioned in writings of 1594, and not completed until 1649.

The surviving portion, begun in 1226, which runs through the college grounds, is kept in order according to an agreement made between the college's founder, William of Wykeham, and the city authorities. This contract has ensured its good repair over the centuries, and there is still an interesting bastion. The wall provides a perfect foil for the mass of flowers along its base, and the velvety green of the lawn. A pamphlet on the college is available at the Holywell Street lodge.

MAGDALEN COLLEGE

Walk through the college as far as you can go through the old buildings, and branch off to the right over a little stone bridge with a wrought-iron gate. You will then be on the tree-lined banks of the Cherwell. The walk round the Water Meadows follows the river all the way round until it arrives back near the colonnaded New Building. Addison's Walk, as it is known, was beloved of the writer Joseph Addison, and was laid out in the sixteenth century. It contains trees not normally associated with the county's river-banks.

In the spring the college is a mass of bulbs and wild flowers, in particular there are the purple fritillaries for which Oxford is famous. The fritillary meadow is grazed after the flowers have finished blooming, and this has helped to spread the growth of the flower.

Between the New Building and Longwall Street is Magdalen Grove, or Deer Park, its trees planted in 1689, its occupants arriving in the early eighteenth century. Before their arrival the Grove was used for drill practice by the University Regiment, and its trees felled for fuel. Luckily for them, the deer are not destined to become venison, for they are 'on the foundation', in other words, members of the college, although at one time it is said, the number of deer equalled that of the Fellows, any additional ones ending up in the dining hall. Traditionally, venison is served at Magdalen's Restoration Dinner in October, the restoration in question being that in 1688 of the college Fellows illegally ejected by James II the year before.

THE UNIVERSITY PARKS

Main access in Parks Road

The Parks were so named because the Royalist artillery was 'parked' there during the Civil War, and they have subsequently been used for drilling in times of war or threat of invasion. Charles II also found them convenient for walking his dogs.

In 1854 the University purchased from Merton College some land to the north of Wadham, as a site for the new University Museum, this being part of fields called the Parks. Over the next few years more Merton land was bought, until the University owned everything between Parks Road and the Cherwell, and in 1865 a walk known as 'Mesopotamia', between the rivers was added. The whole area was laid out and planted as a park in order to create a 'pleasure-ground' which was to be open to the public according to regulations laid down by the University.

In 1880 a cricket ground, complete with pavillion, was constructed and let to the University Cricket Club. Today, this is one of the few places where first-class cricket may be watched free of charge.

The Rainbow Bridge over the Cherwell, paid for by the city, the colleges, and by private individuals, was put up in 1923–4 in order to give work to the unemployed.

The Parks may be closed whenever the curators so decide, and are indeed closed during the two days of St Giles Fair, in early September, although keys may be held by resident members of Convocation.

CHRIST CHURCH MEADOW

Christ Church Meadow may be reached without going into the college itself, either from St Aldate's through the wrought-iron gates, or from Rose Lane off the High Street, beside the Botanic Garden.

It is a large grassy area crossed by several paths, one of which, the Cherwell Walk, follows the river. From this vantage point there is a lovely view of Christ Church itself, with Merton and Magdalen tower. Cherwell Walk also has some of the best spots from which to watch people's attempts at punting, some very skilful, others hilarious.

Part of the land which now forms the meadow was given by Lady Montacute, who lies buried nearby in the Cathedral, for the upkeep of her chantry in the then priory of St Frideswide which occupied the site. At the Dissolution of the Monasteries, the meadow, together with the Priory, became part of Wolsey's Cardinal College, the forerunner of Christ Church.

The meadow is liable to flooding, and was even sailed upon in the nineteenth century, a time when the floods came up as far as the Broad Walk.

In 1965 the meadow became the centre of bitter controversy when plans were afoot to build a road through it to ease Oxford's eternal traffic congestion. Fortunately, the conservationists won the day, and it remains a green haven in the centre of the city, with cattle still grazing on it. Oxford Civic Society has produced a leaflet suggesting both a fifteen-minute and a forty-five-minute walk, complete with a map and descriptions of places of interest en route.

On 'Show Sunday', that before Encaenia, these walks formed a promenade for members of the University and their guests, and indeed for townspeople who wished to see and be seen. This was in the days of Hardy's Jude, and the venue is no longer considered fashionable.

Broad Walk, leading from the Memorial Gardens off St Aldate's to the banks of the Cherwell, is believed to have been made from material excavated when Cardinal College was built. Its avenue of elms, planted in 1668, fell victim to disease and was felled in 1976. Broad Walk was once White Walk, which then became Wide, and then finally Broad. The Poplar Walk, from Meadow Buildings south to the Thames was planted by Dean Liddell, Alice's father, in 1872.

Further along the river are the college boat-houses, descendants of the old college barges, and a meeting-place for supporters of the college crew during Eights Week.

ANGEL AND GREYHOUND MEADOW

This strangely named meadow, which is reached via the streets leading off St Clement's, stretches from the Cherwell where it borders Magdalen to the Marston Road. Its name comes from its use by inns of the same names, as grazing land for their livery stables and coach horses.

ON THE RIVER AT OXFORD

'I tried to work myself up to a little enthusiasm, and took a draught of the water of Isis so much celebrated in poetry, but all in vain.' So wrote James Boswell, the devoted friend of Dr Johnson, in the eighteenth century. He was right to anticipate 'enthusiasm' at the prospect of seeing Oxford's rivers, for they play an important part in the life of both the city and the University.

Oxford is situated at the confluence of the Rivers Thames and Cherwell (pronounced 'Charwell') and intersected by numerous small streams. Confusingly, that section of the Thames which flows between Folly Bridge and Iffley is often called the Isis, in much the same way that the Cam becomes the Granta within the confines of Cambridge.

The Isis is, in fact the most important stretch of river, and constitutes Oxford's race-course. Formerly, college barges lined its banks, but now they have all rotted away to be replaced by more solid and mundane structures on dry land.

For an Oxford oarsperson (for colleges now have a women's eight) the most notable times of the year are February, when 'Torpids' take place, and Eights Week, in late May, when five days are devoted to Bump Races. Eights Week, the more important of the two, is also a social occasion, and forms a wonderful excuse for visits from friends and relations, for dances and concerts, for tea and cucumber sandwiches.

The winning eight becomes Head of the River, and receives a cup for their efforts; a large public house near Folly Bridge has recently been named 'The Head of the River'. Any eight which has done very well will at least consider entering for an event or two at Henley Royal Regatta in July.

'Those who do not shine, or who are not filled with the competitive spirit,' as the *Oxford University Handbook* for 1962 rather dryly puts it, may, nevertheless, enjoy themselves messing about in rowing-boats, punts, canoes, skiffs or pleasure-steamers.

Favourite places for hiring punts, as well as rowing-boats and canoes, are at Old Horse Ford by the side of Magdalen Bridge, and at the Cherwell Boathouse, at the far end of Bardwell Road, off the Banbury Road. In Oxford one punts from the sloping end, and it is sensible to carry a paddle with which to push the punt away from the bank. Nowadays, though, one need not fear the fate which befell a couple of Victorian punters whose skeletons were discovered in the 1920s, in a rotting punt, having spent several decades lost underground in the murky waters of the Trill Mill Stream.

Alice's Adventures in Wonderland were first related here on the river in 1862, by C.L. Dodgson, alias Lewis Carroll, a maths don from Christ Church, and it is hardly surprising that Kenneth Grahame found inspiration in Oxfordshire riverbanks. Rat's descendants continue to plop into the water right beside your craft, but the modern generation of toads has to be helped to safety across the county's roads by kindly ecologists, instead of being themselves Kings of the Open Road.

Oxford is not, however, an advisable place in which to swim or bathe, for the river bottom can be unexpectedly deep and uneven, and the banks dangerous with weed and overhanging branches. Nude bathing was, and sometimes still is, indulged in, which used to cause mutual embarrassment when ladies passed by in boats. Later, females were given their own swimming area, together with a custodian. Today there is nude male bathing at Parson's Pleasure, on the Cherwell, but this is under threat of closure. More conventional swimming is to be had out of doors at Long Bridges, along the Towpath from Folly Bridge, at Tumbling Bay, off the Botley Road, and at Wolvercote, while indoor pools are at Temple Cowley and the Ferry Centre in Summertown.

The University Boat Race

No mention of Oxford rivers would be complete without an account of the most famous sporting event of the University year, the annual Boat Race. So thoroughly has the event entered into the imagination of the general public that it has even passed into Cockney rhyming slang, where 'boat race' means 'face'. It does not, however, take place on either the Cam or the Isis, but on neutral ground in London.

The first race was the result of a challenge issued to Oxford by Cambridge in 1829; Oxford wore dark blue jerseys, later to become the Oxford blue, while their opponents sported pink sashes. Oxford were, on this occasion, both more skilful and stronger. In 1836 Cambridge dressed in white outfits with a light blue ribbon on the bows of their boat, thus adopting their own Cambridge blue.

A course was decided upon between Putney and Mortlake on the Thames at London, and, from 1856 onwards, this became the established course. It is 4½miles long.

Today the race is held in March or early April, the captain of

Monastic 'houses', Worcester College

Front quad, Oriel College

Above: 'Streaky bacon' Gothic, Keble College Chapel. *Below left*: The High Street frontage of Brasenose College. *Below right*: Tom Tower, Christ Church

'The Bridge of Sighs', Hertford
College

Open-air pulpit, Magdalen
College

Deer in Magdalen Grove

Front quad, Worcester College

the previous year's losing team issuing a formal challenge. A coin is tossed to determine who shall take the inner and who the outer bend, a matter of great importance. The coin used is an 1829 sovereign, in memory of the year in which the first race took place, and it was given by John Snagge, the BBC commentator who covered the event for forty-five years.

It is by no means unknown for a crew to sink; Cambridge did so in 1859 and 1878, Oxford in 1925 and 1951, while in 1912 both boats sank. Blackouts were suffered by Oxford men in four races, but by far the most spectacular sight was Cambridge's ramming of a barge in 1984 before they were even under starter's orders. The remnants now have pride of place in a Cambridge pub, displayed on the wall, and signed by all crew members. A note from the cox reads 'All my own work!'

The score to date (1989) is Cambridge 69 Oxford 65, with one dead heat in 1877. Oxford made history in 1981 by choosing the first woman cox, Sue Brown, in their winning crew, and the Dark Blues always take full advantage of their Rhodes Scholars when selecting their eight.

The race is the third most popular event receiving television coverage in the United Kingdom, after the FA Cup Final and the Grand National. The estimated audience worldwide in 1986 was some 150 million people.

7 OXFORD PEOPLE

In 1988 Oxford had already produced 24 Prime Ministers, 24 Nobel Prize winners, and had 1,400 academic staff, including about 150 Professors. There were around 13,500 resident members, of which 75 per cent were undergraduate, 25 per cent graduate. The ratio of men to women was 3:2; of Arts students to Scientists 3:2, and the 2,400 or so overseas students came from 107 different countries, forming 18 per cent of the total student population.

Oxonians through the ages have included men from all walks of life, not all of them noble, many of them not particularly rich. Some have been only too anxious to leave, while Oxford has seen fit to hasten the departure of others. The best-known need no introduction in this book, for their lives and achievements may be found in any encyclopaedia. It would be pointless to write here a potted life history of, say, Sir Christopher Wren, Sir Thomas More, Dr Johnson or Graham Greene. A list of important sons and daughters of the University is included in this chapter, but here too are the lesser known Oxonians, or those who are not immediately associated with the University.

Not forgotten are those benefactors, large and small, who have contributed towards making Oxford what it is today, and whose names live on in its libraries, museums, customs and memories. Alongside such names as Bodley and Sheldon are those of certain characters who are bound to spring up from time to time in such an ancient and eccentric city, most of them real, if not actually famous, but one or two purely imaginary. Fact or fiction, alive or dead, they have all combined to give Oxford its unique atmosphere and are gathered here together to explain to the visitor who and what they once were, and why they are remembered in Oxford today.

Here, then, are benefactors and characters, and royal personages and Prime Ministers, and a whole host of Oxford graduates from eight centuries of our history.

BENEFACTORS

Elias Ashmole

Ashmole was born in Lichfield in 1617 and studied law; in 1638 he became a solicitor. The year 1645 saw him quartered with the Royalist garrison at Oxford, and he was admitted to Brasenose College, where he studied natural philosophy, mathematics and astronomy, as well as writing works on astrology. Other interests were botany and chemistry.

In 1660 he was appointed Windsor Herald, later he was called to the bar, and finally he became a Fellow of the Royal Society.

In 1677 Ashmole gave his collection of curiosities and antiques, many of which had been the property of the Tradescants (see page 130) to the University, and in 1683 the Museum which bears his name was opened in Broad Street to house these treasures; it is the oldest public museum in England, although it is now in a Victorian building in Beaumont Street.

Sir Thomas Bodley

Born in 1545 in Exeter, of a Protestant father who was obliged to flee the country when Mary Tudor came to the throne, Thomas Bodley was educated in Geneva, and then at Magdalen College. Later, he became a Fellow of Merton. Between 1580 and 1597 he worked as a diplomat in various European embassies, but returned to England when he retired, and decided to spend the remainder of his life restoring and refurbishing the sadly depleted University Library, so making it one of the first public libraries in Europe.

Bodley gave a farm in Berkshire, land in London, and most of his money and possessions when he died to the Library which was to be named in his honour; he died a rich man, having had the foresight to marry a wealthy widow. Not only did he put all that he had into the Bodleian, he also canvassed his many friends and colleagues for donations of cash, books and manuscripts, which they gave most generously.

The Library was opened again for use, after a lapse of some fifty years, in November 1602, with a stock of more than 2,000 volumes. Bodley was knighted in 1604, and in 1610 he made an agreement with the Stationers' Company that the Library should receive a copy of each new book printed in the United Kingdom. Nowadays, it is one of six copyright libraries, along with the British Library, Cambridge University Library, Trinity College Dublin Library, and the National Libraries of Scotland and Wales. Bodley started on plans for an eastern extension to be made, but died in January 1613 before they could come to fruition. He is buried in Merton College chapel, and his monument, complete with bust, is on the west wall of the ante-chapel.

His will made provision for a third floor to be built around the proposed quadrangle, now Old Schools Quad, which initially had only two floors.

Today Bodley's library is second in the country only to the British Library, and the appointment of Bodley's Librarian a very prestigious one indeed.

Campaign for Oxford

The Campaign, for fundraising, was launched in the Sheldonian Theatre on 26 October 1988. Among the pledges and donations were £20 million from Squibb, the pharmaceutical company, under a seven-year agreement whereby the Company gets access to any discoveries made, and £3 million from the Rhodes Trust, already a great benefactor to both the University and to Oriel College.

Perhaps the most impressive, though, and one which was duly entered on the balance sheet along with all the rest, was a contribution from a Signorina Maria Paola Ciliberti, of Castellan Grotte, Italy. In a letter to the Vice-Chancellor she writes:

> I am called Maria Paola and I am six years old. Recently my father read in the paper that your college might have to close down because of economic difficulties.
>
>   Because my greatest dream is that one day I will be able to come to your college, I am sending my little contribution to be sure that my dream does not disappear,
> Regards, Maria Paola.

Enclosed was £10.

Edward Hyde, 1st Earl of Clarendon

Edward Hyde was born in 1609, near Salisbury, and educated at Magdalen Hall. He was called to the bar in 1625, and became a Member of Parliament in 1640. At the outbreak of the Civil War he was a moderate royalist, and became Chancellor of the Exchequer in 1643. After the execution of Charles I in 1649, Hyde became one of Charles II's chief advisors during his years in exile.

At the Restoration he was created Baron, and in 1661, Earl of Clarendon. He managed to marry his daughter Anne to James, Duke of York, later James II, but was an unpopular minister because he was too staunch an Anglican to satisfy Catholics and non-conformists. Altogether he cut a very pompous figure at the court of the Merry Monarch, and in 1667 was forced to resign his Chancellorship of England due to adverse public opinion, caused in part by the country's lack of success in the wars with the Dutch. Clarendon was also impeached, but not convicted.

He went abroad for the rest of his life, and finished his work, the *History of the Great Rebellion*. This was published in 1702–4, after his death, which occurred in 1674. Perpetual copyright was given to the University by his son, in order to help finance the Clarendon Press. The book is obviously a prejudiced account of the Civil War years but is none the less a valuable contemporary insight into seventeenth-century England. Clarendon is buried in Westminster Abbey.

In Oxford the name of Clarendon lives on, not only in the Building and Press of that name, but also in a laboratory, an institute, a guide to Oxford, two streets, a club, and a shopping centre.

William Laud

Laud was born in Reading, the son of a cloth merchant. He was educated at Reading Free School and later at St John's College, where he became a Fellow in 1593, at the age of twenty. He was ordained in 1601, gained a doctorate in Divinity in 1608, and then various appointments in the Church until, in 1628, he became Bishop of London, and powerful at the court of Charles I. In 1630 he was elected Chancellor of Oxford University, and three years later Archbishop of Canterbury.

Laud was a severe Anglican and made the mistake of underestimating the force of non-conformist opinion against him. He was a great supporter of Charles I, whom he urged to resist the demands of his subjects. In 1640 Laud was impeached for high treason by the Long Parliament, and sent to the Tower of London. After a trial for high treason in 1644, he was beheaded in 1645. Laud's *Diary* was published in 1695.

Although, in many ways, Laud can be said to be largely responsible for the tragedy of the Civil War, he was very concerned for the good of the University which he loved, and drew up the Laudian Code of reforms in order that it might become more efficient.

He ordered Statutes to be drawn up by Brian Twyne, first Keeper of the University Archives. These reviewed the entire University system of government and study, without departing any further than was strictly necessary from the traditional ways and the old Statutes.

When he was at the peak of his career in 1636, Laud assisted his old college by paying for new buildings, including the library;

this was also a year in which Charles I visited Oxford. Until this benefaction, St John's had not been a wealthy college, but, following his help, it became one of the greatest in the University.

Despite Laud's fall, his code lived on, and is apparent even today, particularly in academic dress, which was defined by him. Examples and samples of material were submitted for reference under Title XIV which ordered Heads of House to determine the correct form of each gown, with a copy of each to be stored in a special chest.

William Richard Morris

A Worcester boy by birth, Morris grew up in Cowley, where he went to the local school. At the age of sixteen he began a business, repairing bicycles in a shed, and later progressing to motor-bikes. His first car was produced in 1911, and the following year he opened up a factory in Oxford's Longwall Street.

The first Morris Cowley revolutionized the British car market, making ownership within the reach of the ordinary man. This model was on sale at £165, and was made at Morris's new, larger factory in the former Military College at Cowley. During the Great War the factory changed to making mine-sinkers, but by 1920 it was doing good business in mass-produced cars.

Morris was created Baronet in 1929, Baron in 1934 and 1st Viscount Nuffield in 1938, a year before his millionth car was sold. In 1927 he bought Wolseley Motors Ltd, and went on to absorb the Riley company. In 1952 Morris and Austin merged to form the British Motor Corporation, with Morris as Chairman. By 1938 he had given £11,500,000 towards research, education and charity, and of this amount £3,128,000 had been donated to the University, in the form of professorships of medicine, and, in 1937, Nuffield College.

In 1943 a further £10 million went to the Nuffield Trust and Foundation for medical research and services, studies in trade and industry, and social sciences. Lord Nuffield was made an

Honorary MA and then Doctor of Civil Law, in recognition of his services. He and his wife lived at Nuffield Place, near Henley on Thames, from 1933 until his death thirty years later.

John Radcliffe

Oxonians who hear the words 'John Radcliffe' will immediately think of the hospital rather than the man after which it is named. Radcliffe was born in Yorkshire in 1650, and went to grammar school in Wakefield, then on to University College at the age of thirteen. He took his BA, then his BM, and became a Fellow of Lincoln College in 1669. He began his medical practice in Oxford, with a new approach to medicine, replacing the old blood-letting and superstition with a no-nonsense attitude based on attention to the patient's general health and ability to combat disease. Even Hearne, that critic of the famous, seems to have approved of him. In 1684 Radcliffe moved from Oxford to London, where he was even more successful, numbering among his patients the aristocracy and even members of the royal family.

He attended the Princess Anne, but offended her by refusing to interrupt a party to come to see her. She turned to a competitor of Radcliffe's, who eventually failed to cure the heir to the throne of typhoid, so ushering in the House of Hanover on the death of Queen Anne.

Radcliffe was not over-popular with the polite element of London society thanks to his blunt Northern ways and refusal to toady to their whims. He died in 1714 and left £40,000 to pay for a physic library at Oxford, the results being the Radcliffe Camera. The money was only released by his trustees in 1736, the foundation stone laid in 1737, and the building completed in 1749. Radcliffe also left money towards the extending of St Bartholomew's Hospital in London, and for travelling medical fellowships. Money from his estate went towards the Radcliffe Infirmary which opened in 1770.

The Radcliffe Observatory, in the grounds of Green College, was begun by Keene in 1772, and finished by Wyatt. Above the windows are the signs of the Zodiac. Here too, are the Winds with their Greek names, and Hercules and Atlas supporting a copper-covered globe. The JR II Hospital, on a 75-acre site at Headington, largely replaces the old Infirmary; its first phase, the Maternity Unit, was built 1968–72.

Cecil Rhodes

Cecil John Rhodes was born in Bishop's Stortford in 1853, and in 1869, owing to poor health, went to Natal to work with his brother on a cotton plantation. In 1873 he returned to England, and went up to Oriel College, already a successful businessman, only to fall ill once more and leave. In 1881 he finally took his degree. By 1874 he had amassed a large holding in the diamond fields of Kimberley, and in 1880 he combined several small companies to make the De Beer Mining Company.

Rhodes's political aim was to make a South African federation into a valuable part of the British Empire, and he became involved with the country's government. In 1899 came the Boer War.

Rhodes died in 1902, and was buried, as he wished, in the Matopo Hills. In his will, his house, Groote Schuur, was left to the prime ministers of South Africa as a residence, and he has a memorial on the slopes of Table Mountain.

Nearer home, if one looks up in King Edward Street, one can see a portrait and memorial to Rhodes above Shepherd and Woodward's shop. The Rhodes Scholarships (see page 73) were valued at £300 each, and today more than eighty Rhodes Scholars receive a two-year scholarship at Oxford.

Gilbert Sheldon

Sheldon was born in 1598, at Ashbourne, Derbyshire, the son of Roger Sheldon of Stanton, Staffordshire. He came up to Trinity College in 1614, took his BA in 1617, his MA in 1620, and was incorporated at Cambridge the previous year. In 1622 he was made a Fellow of All Souls, and Warden in 1626. Two years later he took his BD and in 1634 his Doctorate in Divinity. He held various livings, including some small ones in Oxfordshire.

Strongly anti-Puritan in his religious views, Sheldon was a friend of Clarendon, and supported him in parliament. In 1648 Sheldon was ejected from the wardenship of All Souls by parliamentarian visitors, and was taken to Oxford gaol, but set free at the end of that year on condition that he did not come within five miles of either Oxford or the Isle of Wight, where Charles I was at the time. Sheldon retired to his native Midlands for the time being, and was reinstated as Warden of All Souls in 1659, shortly before the Restoration. In 1660 he was made Bishop of London, and, in 1663, Archbishop of Canterbury.

The new Archbishop believed that Oxford degree ceremonies, or the 'Act' as they were then called, were totally unsuitable for St Mary the Virgin Church in which they were then held, and resolved to start an appeal for a secular assembly hall for University use. The result was the Sheldonian Theatre, started to plans by Wren in 1664, and opened in 1669, at a cost of well over £14,000, the vast majority of which was given by Sheldon himself. In addition, he bought lands worth £2,000 to 'support the fabrick' of the Theatre.

In 1667, Sheldon was elected Chancellor of Oxford, but was never sworn in or installed, and resigned in July, shortly after the opening of his Theatre. He never saw the building, for, by then, he was at Lambeth, and did not come to the opening celebrations.

In addition to the money given to the University, Sheldon also encouraged the rebuilding of St Paul's Cathedral, and donated more than £4,000 towards the project. It was estimated that his total gifts to charity and other worthwhile causes over his lifetime amounted to about £72,000, a stupendous sum for those days.

Sheldon died at Lambeth in November 1677, and was buried at Croydon, where his nephew, Sir Joseph Sheldon, Lord Mayor of London, erected a monument to his memory. Gilbert Sheldon never married.

The Two John Tradescants

John the Elder was a botanist and antiquarian who was born somewhere in East Anglia, but it is not certain exactly when or where. In 1609 he entered into the service of Robert Cecil, 1st Earl of Salisbury, at Hatfield House.

John travelled extensively in the Netherlands and France, collecting plants for the grounds and gardens at Hatfield, and besides his botanical specimens he returned with 'rarities' or novelties, then looked upon as the scientific discoveries of the day. With no media and very little general distribution of books, our ancestors were forced to collect such souvenirs as a Turkish toothbrush in place of today's travel guides and reference books! Later Tradescant worked for Lord Wotton, and travelled as far afield as the Mediterranean countries, and even Moscow, where he took the opportunity of collecting yet more specimens and rarities.

In 1623 he went to work for George Villiers, Duke of Buckingham, and went with him when the Duke brought Henrietta Maria to England as a bride for the future Charles I. As always, rarities and plants came back with them.

In 1630 John was appointed Keeper of His Majesty's Gardens, Vines and Silkworms at Oatlands Palace in Surrey, and then first Custodian of the Botanic Garden at Oxford, but he died in 1631 before he could take up the position.

John Tradescant Junior was born in 1608, and became a great traveller. In 1637 he made the first of three visits to Virginia, gathering flowers, plants, shells and further rarities, and brought back Powhatan's Mantle, Powhatan was the Red Indian King of Virginia, and the father of Pocohontas. After his father's death, John was appointed Keeper at Oatlands, and his portrait in the Ashmolean shows him as a working gardener.

Together, the Tradescants brought back many of the trees, flowers and shrubs common in Britain today. Their collections went to form the nucleus of the Ashmolean Museum, and other specimens are in the Bodleian, the University Museum, and the Pitt Rivers Collection. Their joint collections were presented, with his own, by Elias Ashmole in 1677.

CHARACTERS

An obituary in *Jackson's Oxford Journal* of 13 November 1818 reads:

> On Saturday last aged 81, died Mrs Rebecca Howse. Under the name of Mother Goose, and as a seller of Flowers, Water Cresses, and other excellent vegetables, she has been well known for a long series of years to every resident in this place and neighbourhood.
>
> She attended the principal Inns, and was admitted to a sort of privileged familiarity with a number of distinguished persons in their occasional visits to the University, from whom she seldom failed to profit from their benevolence.

And another, from the *Journal* of 16 January 1830:

> Tuesday last died, aged about 60, William Saunders of St Thomas's in this city, better known by the appellation of 'Billy on the Stool'. He was an idiot, perfectly harmless and, having lost the use of his legs, was accustomed for years to travel through our streets on a low joint-stool.
>
> Billy has, in several instances, been introduced by artists into their drawings of buildings in this city as a well-known character in the streets.

There is, in Wadham College, a portrait of an Oxford character who has nothing at all to do with that College. The picture was presented by the artist van Sonman, in recognition of hospitality received there. The subject was known as 'Mother George', and her picture shows her to have fine hands, which she carefully displays. Mother George died in July 1691, at a great, but unknown, age.

John Locke, the philosopher, saw her in 1682, and remarked that she had a 'comely face' and claimed to be 108 years old. This estimate would have made her 118 when she died; other versions say 111, or 120. Anthony à Wood wrote that 'when she came to be 100 she doubled every year'. All that seems to be known about her is that she married at thirty, and produced fifteen children. Her usual means of support in her extreme old age was to thread a needle without wearing glasses, for which feat she received a gratuity.

C. L. Dodgson

In 1832, Charles Lutwidge Dodgson was born at Daresbury, Cheshire. Even as a child he wrote stories and arranged entertainment for his seven sisters and one brother. He was educated at Rugby and then went up to Oxford in 1851, to read Mathematics at Christ Church, where he got a First in 1854. He was to spend the rest of his life at the College, becoming a Lecturer in 1855, and taking Deacon's orders in 1861. Dodgson was shy, and inclined to stammer, which could explain why he felt more at home in the company of children who judged him on his individual merits. Photography sessions and boating trips on the Thames made up his 'white stone' or red-letter days in their company, his particular favourites being the children at the Christ Church Deanery, the Liddells. Dodgson was an early portrait photographer of Ruskin, Tennyson, and Rossetti, among other famous men of his time. He fixed up a photographic studio on the roof of his room in Tom Quad, and some of his equipment is housed in the Museum of the History of Science. He enjoyed playing with words, and made the characters in the stories which he wrote for the three Liddell sisters indulge in nonsense conversations, full of puns and topical references.

His friends, when they read the manuscript edition of *Alice's Adventures Underground* urged him to publish. This appeared, published by Macmillan, as *Alice's Adventures in Wonderland* in 1865, under the pen-name of Lewis Carroll. Dodgson continued to publish mathematical treatises under his own name, and was a little sensitive about his 'double life'. The sequel to the first Alice book, *Alice Through the Looking-Glass*, which came out in 1871, was much more sophisticated than its predecessor, as it was intended for publication from the beginning. Both books originally had illustrations by Tenniel, one of which is the 'Sheep Shop' in St Aldate's where Alice herself used to buy barleysugars. All of Dodgson's work, including the nonsense poem *The Hunting of the Snark* (1876) may be read as fun, nonsense, allegory, or satire, depending on one's views. Dodgson died in 1898 during a visit to his sister in Guildford.

In 1948 the original manuscript of *Alice* was given to the British Museum by the Librarian of Congress, Dr Luther H. Evans, as 'a gift from America to the British people' at the end of a hard and bitter war. It had fetched $50,000 at auction.

The final accolade came when Dodgson's old college put an 'Alice' window into hall, along with his own portrait which was already there. The window gives his date and place of birth and death, with pictures of, among others, the White Rabbit, the Dodo, the March Hare, the Mad Hatter, the Dormouse, the Queen and the Duchess, the Griffin, the Mock Turtle, the Caterpillar, the Whiting and the Cheshire Cat.

Thomas Hearne

Thomas, the son of George Hearne, parish clerk of White Waltham, Berkshire, was born in 1678 and came up to St Edmund Hall when he was seventeen. At Oxford he proved a very moral and studious young man, and took his BA in 1699.

Already a frequenter of the Bodleian Library, he was appointed Assistant Keeper in 1701, and was promoted to Second Keeper in 1712. In 1715, however, he was 'debarr'd upon account of the oaths'; in other words, Hearne lost his position because he was a confirmed supporter of the Stuart cause, and refused to take the oath of allegiance to the House of Hanover. The Bodleian Library even had its lock changed so that he might not gain admittance, so Hearne went back to St Edmund Hall, where he began to publish, having been writing for several years previously. Between 1705 and 1735 he filled 145 small notebooks with notes suited to his position as scholar and librarian, with much material concerning the history of the University, and comments on contemporary events and persons, rather in the manner of Anthony à Wood the previous century. Like Wood before him, Hearne became troublesome to certain senior members of the University, and was seen as dangerous for his anti-Hanoverian attitude, as a general trouble-maker, and as a fool to himself, for he was indiscreet.

It is these very indiscretions which make him such a valuable source of information for students of everyday life in eighteenth-century Oxford, for he hides nothing, whether he is talking of world-wide events, or the minutiae of college life. He made a living by his own efforts at writing and publishing, and after he died on 10 June 1735, more than £1,000 was found in his room.

Here is Hearne on G.F. Handel:

> July 8th 1733: another Performance at 5/- a ticket, in the Theater by Mr Handel for his own benefit, continuing till about 8 o'clock. NB his book (not worth 1d.) he sells for 1s.

And on a tragedy at the Clarendon Building:

> January 8th 1714: Death of Mr John Clarke of an Hectick Feaver ... He catched his Death by the New Printing House, which, being at present, a very cold, damp Place, several of the Printers have since their Removal thither, fallen into Sickness.

And on Teddy Hall:

> 22nd February 1726: Last Night began to be emptied Edmund Hall Bog-House, which no body that I know of remembers to have been emptied. They worked but one Night, the Principal, upon consideration, ordering them to desist.

Jude the Obscure and Oxford

Jude the Obscure, Thomas Hardy's last novel, was published in 1896, the same year as Oscar Wilde's *The Importance of being Earnest*. Hardy's book had the distinction of being burned by the Bishop of Wakefield, who succeeded in getting it banned from Smith's Circulating Library as immoral. Hardy shows us both sides of the Oxford coin, firstly through the idealism of the young Jude who is still living with his aunt in the Berkshire Downs. His view is confirmed by the description of the place by a local labourer (who, incidentally, freely admits that he has never been there) as being full of learning, music, and religion: 'they raise pa'sons there like radishes in a bed'. To Jude, at this stage, the voice of the city is the sound of bells carried on the breeze. 'Christminster', as Hardy calls Oxford, is still, at least superficially, a Christian city; indeed Sue, Jude's cousin, and later his lover, earns her living by illuminating extracts from the Bible.

Hardy knew all too well, though, the other Oxford, with its sour-smelling, poverty-stricken courts and alleyways, all very un-Arnold, and easy prey to cholera. He also understood the love-hate relationship between Town and Gown, for, although Jude desperately wants to be accepted by a college, he is not averse to being an early graffitist and chalking his comments on the wall of the college which offers him excellent but unwanted advice. Hardy himself worked in Oxford, as assistant architect under Blomfield, who was building St Barnabas' church, in the very working-class suburb of Jericho, between 1867 and 1870. 'Barni' church comes into the novel as 'St Silas'.

Many other Oxford names are there in disguise: Biblioll for Balliol, Cardinal for Christ Church, Remembrance Day for Commemoration, Fourways for Carfax, and so on. Jude lodges in Beersheba, thinly disguised Jericho. Some of the sights of Oxford appear as themselves. Jude surveys the promised land of academe from the 'octagonal chamber in the lantern of a singularly-built theatre' and so may we if we climb up to the cupola of the Sheldonian. Outside are the heads of the 'Emperors', 'frost eaten and much decayed', although they had been replaced in 1868. Jude is saddened by the state of the buildings, some of the colleges appearing to be like 'vaults above ground', and Mildew Lane and Sarcophagus College speak for themselves. Nevertheless, our hero is fascinated by all this Gothic.

A picture is given us of the amount of interest shown by Town when anything noteworthy is being done by Gown, such as the

Bump Races or Commemoration Week. Country people brought picnics to eat in college gardens and quads, as if they were visiting a stately home, and Jude's stone-worker mates go off to the river, while he is dying on a fine summer's afternoon. Altogether Hardy manages to convey this strange mixture of privilege and poverty, from the young gentlemen and their dainty ladies taking tea in college, to the labourers and light ladies of the Beersheba pubs. In all, modern Victoriana mixes with medieval relics to produce a claustrophobic, unwholesome atmosphere.

Hardy was given an honorary Doctorate of Literature in 1921, and was an Honorary Fellow of the Queen's College, being entertained there during the last year of his life; thus Jude may be said to have gained his degree in the end.

Katherine Martyr

Katherine was the German wife of Peter Martyr, a Protestant from Florence, who fled to England in 1547 at the invitation of Cranmer. Peter became Regius Professor of Divinity the year after he arrived, and, in 1550, a Canon of Christ Church. The couple's stay at Christ Church was not a happy one, though, for they were plagued by Catholic students who broke their windows and disturbed their slumbers. Finally, Peter was driven away at the accession of Queen Mary. Katherine, his wife, was already dead by then, and buried in Christ Church.

An enquiry instigated by Cardinal Pole in 1554 discovered that Katherine had been buried near St Frideswide, in the Cathedral. As she had not spoken English, no-one knew if Mrs Martyr had been Catholic or Protestant, so the Cardinal decided that it was too risky to permit her to remain there, and 'ut quoniam juxta corpus sanctissimae Frideswidae jacebat corpus Petri Martyris exhumari et jactari faciat', so out she went. Accordingly, her corpse was dug up, carried to a dung-heap belonging to the intruded Dean, put into the Cathedral by Bloody Mary, and reburied there.

In the dung-heap lay Katherine until Mary died, Elizabeth

came to the throne, and Dean Marshall himself was removed. Orders came to Christ Church for an honorable reburial, and a search-party was sent to the Dean's stable-yard to recover Katherine's body. The remains were collected up, and left until a feast-day. About this time, by curious coincidence, some more bones, wrapped in silk, were discovered in a dark corner of the Cathedral. These were declared to be those of St Frideswide, which, before the Reformation, had been put on display on important feast-days, near to the high altar.

After a good deal of discussion, both ladies were popped into a shared grave, with due pomp and ceremony, on 11 January 1562, thus satisfying both Catholics and Protestants that their own lady would be safe, owing to the intermingling of the bones. A volume of Latin poems was composed in celebration of the occasion.

Inspector Morse

The creator of Inspector Morse, Colin Dexter, is a Cambridge graduate who was a Classics master for fourteen years. In 1966 he came to work in Oxford at the Oxford Delegacy for Local Examinations. Oxford is both the inspiration and setting for the Inspector Morse detective novels, which have been made into films for television, starring John Thaw in the title role, with Kevin Whately as his side-kick, Sergeant Lewis. Local Oxford people, some of them members of drama groups, are roped in as extras in the series. Morse has now become the most popular detective on television, with fifteen million viewers for the first series. The first Morse novel, *Last Bus to Woodstock* was, in fact, written in Wales.

Although Colin Dexter has done his homework very thoroughly, he freely admits to not having researched in depth on police procedures. Disguises are necessary for both people and places in Oxford, and one of the attractions for Oxonians is playing the game of 'spot the college'. Some venues prove to be a mixture of two or more places, just to fool the audience.

The episodes of *Morse* are filmed in and around Oxford, and the maroon Jaguar car and John Thaw himself, are common enough sights in the city. Some Morse stories have been specially written for television, such as *The Wolvercote Tongue*. Colin Dexter appears, briefly, in some episodes, as does Dr Robert Gasser, Bursar of Brasenose, who acts as go-between for the film-crew, and who himself holds an Equity card!

Nathaniel, Lord Crewe

Nathaniel Crewe came up to Lincoln College in 1652, and took his BA three years later. While he was up at Oxford he made himself very popular by his hospitality, for he was a rich and open-handed youth. In 1658 he took his MA, and was 'Senior Inceptor' that year, that is first on the list of MAs. This was a most expensive position to be in, for it involved entertaining the Heads of Houses, Proctors, Doctors and other senior members of the University at a banquet, financed by the candidate. The Senior Inceptor each year was chosen by the Proctors from those who could afford this honour. Crewe held his 'Vesper Supper' in the Hall of his college, and it was voted a great success by all who attended. His father was made a peer at the Restoration, which added to his son's already considerable prestige at Lincoln.

In 1663, as Senior Proctor, Nathaniel welcomed Charles II to Oxford, and he was given an honorary doctorate of Civil Law the following year, by request of Gilbert Sheldon. Crewe became Rector of Lincoln in 1668 and, in 1671, Bishop of Oxford. The next year, however, he resigned the Rectorship to become Bishop of Durham.

Although Crewe appears to have been something of a time-server as regards his political activities, there is no doubt that he cared deeply for his college and was most generous towards it. He died on 18 September 1722, and is buried in his home parish of Stene, Northamptonshire. Among the bequests mentioned in his will are funds for the endowment of the Creweian Oration, spoken during Encaenia, and the Creweian

Benefaction consumed before it. As stated in the 1969 Oration: 'Nathaniel, Lord Crewe enjoined on us, with an endowment of £200 per annum, the celebration of our benefactors, himself included, with strawberries and champagne.'

Warden Spooner of New College

William Archibald Spooner was born in 1844, an albino with weak eyesight. He went to Oswestry School, and, against long odds owing to his disability, won an open scholarship to New College in 1862. He had the distinction of being the first non-Wykehamist scholar to be elected, for previously all members of New College had to come from William of Wykeham's twin foundation at Winchester.

Spooner soon made himself popular by his cheerful personality and interest in everything, and took a First in literae humaniores in 1866. A Fellowship followed in 1867, a Lectureship the next year, and Tutorship in 1869; he finally became Dean in 1876, a position which he was to hold for thirteen years. He lectured in Ancient History, Philosophy and Divinity, and became a deacon in 1872, a priest in 1875, and Doctor of Divinity in 1903, the year in which he was unanimously elected Warden of New College.

Spooner is remembered for the improvements which were made to the College in his time, and for his attitude of treating members of the College as individuals. For upwards of seventy years he was one of Oxford's best-loved characters, and when he died in 1930 he was sadly missed.

It is not as an academic, however, that the outside world tends to remember Warden Spooner, but for the delightful 'Spoonerisms' which he is said to have made, and which have passed into Oxford folklore.

Many of the so-called examples of spoonerisms were invented by junior members of New College, and doubtless many more have been created since his day. The only one to which Spooner himself admitted was the announcement of the hymn title

'Kinquering Congs their titles take'; strangely enough, said his family, there was never any reason to give out the names of hymns in chapel, for hymnsheets were always provided. Spooner himself referred to his creations as 'those things' and seems to have had some difficulty in reading out loud. His sermons were likely to prove difficult, but he was always a good extempore speaker. The more ambitious of the so-called spoonerisms include:

'I remember your name perfectly, but I just can't think of your face'
'Let us drink to the queer old Dean.' (Perhaps this one was not a mistake at all!), and, worst of all:
'Sir, you have tasted two whole worms, you have hissed all my mystery lectures and been caught fighting a liar in the quad.; you will leave Oxford by the next town drain.

Spooner's mistakes, according to a later Warden, Sir William Hayter, are more like transpositions of ideas, than of initial letters; it is also highly likely that he 'created' situations, sometimes for his own advantage. Julian Huxley remembers his saying 'from Land's End to John of Gaunt', but surely the worst must have been the time when the Warden passed a widow, dressed in full mourning. He turned to his companion, and announced that the poor soul's husband had recently been eaten by missionaries!

Henry Taunt

Henry Taunt was something of a local historian, as he did not confine his photography to commissioned work. His interests were catholic, including as they did street-scenes, countryside, buildings, and above all, the river, which he loved, and near which he spent a good deal of time. Apart from photography, he was a children's entertainer, printer, glass-seller, lecturer, bicycle repairer and seller, as well as being interested in the Druids, politics, botany and music!

Taunt started his career at the age of fourteen with the Oxford photographer Edward Bracher, and by the 1860s was producing his own pictures. By 1869 he had his own shop in the Cornmarket, specializing in the 'Shilling Series' of views of Oxford. Three years later, his first book the *New Map of the River Thames* appeared and Taunt dressed the part with cap and sweater.

At the end of the Great War he wrote 'all photographs have some limited historical value; those taken today will many of them be much wanted in fifty years' time', a prophecy which was to put him on a level with Hearne and Wood as a local historian, although one with a much more immediate appeal.

From taking the everyday sights of his town, Taunt progressed to photographing the 9th Duke of Marlborough, Sir Winston Churchill, and one of his favourite, Blenheim Palace.

By the 1920s, however, there were cameras in many homes and the heyday of the professional photographer of daily life was over as people began to take their own pictures. Taunt was to complain that Kodak's popularity was damaging his own business.

He died in 1922, leaving his house and possessions to Fanny Miles, his housekeeper, and probably his mistress. Much of his equipment was destroyed; then local historian Harry Paintin contacted the City Library, which bought up the surviving negatives and the rest of his equipment in 1924–5. The collection is available in the Central Library's Local History Collections in the Westgate, and leading examples have been reproduced for sale there and in branch libraries. These appear in packs of six, on various themes such as Education, Customs, Markets, or Agriculture. The Collection's own local historian, Dr Malcolm Graham, has written a life of Henry Taunt, with many illustrations from the photographer's own work.

THE STATUES OF OXFORD

For a city which has had such long-lasting connections with the rich and famous, Oxford has surprisingly few statues to their memory. On second thoughts, perhaps it is this enormous number of illustrious associations which has made both City and University so selective, being spoiled for choice. Furthermore, many of the best-loved statuary is of people and things who have no direct link with the place at all, indeed, some of them defy identification.

The so-called 'Emperors', for example, who guard the boundaries of the Sheldonian Theatre and the Museum of the History of Science, are nobody in particular, even though they are some of Oxford's famous faces. Their smaller relations, the corbels and gargoyles which decorate many colleges, notably Magdalen, New College, St Edmund Hall, Brasenose, and also the Bodleian Library, can sometimes be identified, by those who know the original sitters, as local worthies, such as dons, bursars, architects, Heads of House, and their pets! Others, the vast majority, are almost Chaucerian in their portrayal of medieval life, showing craftsmen, fairytale and pantomime characters, mythological beasts, amusing situations, musicians, and animals in human form. However, most of these figures are of fairly recent origin, either due to twentieth-century restoration, or as a result of the Victorians carrying on the 'Gothic' tradition.

There are very few free-standing commemorative statues in Oxford, and most are hidden from the public gaze, or way up over doorways where they are not immediately obvious.

Shelley, for example, lies in his own dome-like memorial in University College, slightly effeminate, reclining above mourning Muses. The Muses themselves live high on the roof of the Clarendon Building in Broad Street. Seven of the nine were made by Thornhill, and put up in November 1717 after having lain 'at ye wharf for two years having been first of all refused.' As Hearne tells us.

Later, however, both Melpomène and Euterpe came to grief, and in 1974, Richard Blackwell, of the bookselling family, donated replacements. The two new Muses, this time made of fibreglass covered with a mixture of lead powder and resin, instead of the lead of the other seven, were welcomed to the Clarendon Building, by a special ceremony held in the Sheldonian Theatre next door.

The Terrae Filius was reintroduced after a lapse of two centuries, but only under the most respectable of circumstances, and the Vice-Chancellor was present. The overture to Handel's 'Athalia' and Haydn's 'Oxford' Symphony were both played, and Latin speeches delivered from, and about, the newcomers. These were designed by Richard Kindersley.

On the west wall of the Clarendon Building, clutching a copy of his *History of the Great Rebellion* and attended by pigeons, stands the Earl of Clarendon, made by Francis Bird about 1721 at a cost of £55. He has earned his position there by donating the cash for the Building from the proceeds of his book, the copyright of which was given to the University for ever. It was not until the third edition, though that the money was forthcoming, that from the first two having been misappropriated by the Vice Chancellor of the time.

Nearby, in Old Schools Quad, the Earl of Pembroke stands guard over the entrance to the Bodleian Library. Once he was among the attractions of the Bodleian picture gallery, snug and warm indoors, but now he spends winter and summer outside. The Earl appears to have the wrong head, perhaps an old one once owned by Charles I. It is a little too small for the body, but can be adjusted to give Pembroke a varied outlook.

Along New College Lane, and in the College ante-chapel is Epstein's 'Lazarus' he who once gave Khrushchev a sleepless night after a visit during the 1950s. Lazarus is a tortuous figure, escaping from the confines of his grave-clothes, but he is one of the characters of New College, and is missed immediately he goes missing. Once, when his place was vacant, the College had so many enquiries as to his whereabouts, that they had to write a notice to the effect that, although he had indeed risen from the dead, Lazarus had only gone as far as London, where he was taking part in an exhibition!

Another favourite is the figure of Mercury, poised in the middle of the pool in Christ Church's Tom Quad. A copy of the

statue by Giovanni da Bologna, Mercury is usually surrounded
by giant carp. Recently, some louts put bleach into the pool and
killed them all off, although Mercury is still there, above all that
sort of thing.

Although founders and benefactors are to be seen as part of
the decor of many of the colleges, Chichele above All Souls,
Wykeham above New College gateway, Rhodes in a niche in his
building at Oriel, Oxford is much richer in portraits than in
statues.

If you wish to see what any great Oxford man looked like,
from the Middle Ages onwards, go to his college, and you are
almost certain to find his portrait in Hall or Chapel, or Common
Room. The Bodleian Library too, still retains its pictures,
although they are not displayed as formerly, as in a gallery. In
both the New and the Old Libraries, there is a series of famous
Oxford men, including most of the founders of colleges prior to
1670 when the series was executed.

ROYALTY AND OXFORD

Traditionally, Oxford has been unlucky for royalty and, at
times, it must have seemed that this was indeed the case for
several sovereigns. Frideswide, who died around 735 had been
pestered by Prince Algar hereabouts, and was forced to retire to
a nunnery; Edmund Ironside, son of Ethelred, was murdered in
Oxford in 1016, and Harold Harefoot, son of Canute, died here
in 1040. Other Saxon royals stayed at their palace in
Headington, within the city boundaries, but seem to have come
to no harm.

At one time, every child knew how in 1142 Mathilda, who
was beseiged in Oxford Castle by her cousin Stephen, slipped
over its walls, clad entirely in white, and made her way over the
snowy fields and along the frozen Thames to Wallingford Castle
and safety.

Henry I built Beaumont Palace, on the site of what is now
Beaumont Street, where Richard the Lionheart was born. Here
too, almost certainly, his hated brother John first saw the light.
All that remains of the Palace today are a few fragments of

windows and hundreds of pigeons, the descendants of the
Palace's winter food supply.

In Queen's College library is a highly painted statue of
Philippa of Hainault, Queen of Edward III, probably
seventeenth-century, and similar to those royal funeral effigies
on display at Westminster Abbey. Philippa was the Queen after
whom the College was named, and her husband praised Oxford
for its contribution to both learning and service to the country.

Henry V stands above All Souls gateway, along with many of
the souls lost in the Hundred Years War against France; he was
at Queen's, and his brother, Humfrey, Duke of Gloucester, gave
many priceless manuscripts to the University Library. These
were housed in the specially built Duke Humfrey's Library, now
a reading-room of the Bodleian.

Edward IV visited Oxford in 1481, entering by way of
Woodstock, and his statue is on Magdalen's Founder's Tower.

Henry VII's mother, the saintly and learned Lady Margaret
Beaufort, founded chairs at both Oxford and Cambridge, and
Lady Margaret Hall is named after her. Henry VIII carried on
this royal tradition, refounding Wolsey's Cardinal College at
Christ Church, and himself endowing five Regius Professorships,
those of Divinity, Civil Law, Medicine, Hebrew and Greek,
each with a yearly stipend of £40. Henry's first wife, Catherine
of Aragon, visited both Christ Church and Binsey well, possibly
in the hope of conceiving a son, on trips to Oxford.

Queen Elizabeth took great interest in her father's foundation,
visiting it in 1566, and again in 1592.

James I, also a great patron of learning in his own peculiar
way, was heard to declare that, were he not king, he would wish
to be an Oxford man. In Old Schools Quad he may be seen to
this day, perched on the top of the Tower of the Five Orders,
and flanked by statues of Learning and Fame. James augmented
some of the endowments of the Regius Professorships in 1605
and 1617, as did his son, Charles I, in 1630.

Charles's stay was to be prolonged in Oxford, possibly longer
than he intended, for he made Oxford his capital when London
was lost to him during the Civil War. The University gave both

Charles and his nephew, Prince Rupert of the Rhine, honorary doctorates in Civil Law, probably the start of this practice. Charles lodged at Christ Church, his queen, Henrietta Maria, next door at Merton, in the Queens' Lodgings there. Both King and Queen remain at St John's College in statue form, no takers being found when they were put up for sale, because of their low bronze content.

Their son, Charles II, also used Oxford as his capital, because the plague had driven the Court from London; his queen too, Katherine of Braganza, lodged at Merton. Charles even had a child born in that college, but not to his wife; the mother was Barbara Castlemaine. These proud parents must have attended the wedding of another of their offspring, Charlotte Fitzroy, to one of the Lee family, at Spelsbury church, in west Oxfordshire. Yet another of Charles's children, the eldest, James, Duke of Monmouth, son of Lucy Walter, was at Corpus.

Charles himself, attired like an ancient Roman, stands over the Danby Gate of the Botanic Garden. In 1680, though, Oxonians were able to view the real thing, for Charles himself came from Windsor, and was met at the East Gate by the University and City dignitaries. This time both King and Queen stayed at Christ Church.

Parliament was due to meet on 21 March 1680, with the King presiding over the Lords. This went well, but on the 28th Charles came into the Lords, dressed in his royal robes, having already sent for the Commons. He told them that he 'could expect no good success of this Parliament', and promptly dissolved it; he returned to London the same day. The following year, he was back again, this time on a royal visit. Now the Lords were housed in the School of Geometry, the Commons packed into Convocation House. Charles made incognito visits to the Sheldonian, to the Bodleian, and to the Tower of the Five Orders to see 'exact effigies' of his grandfather, James I.

Charles's brother James II did not appreciate the ceiling painting in the Sheldonian Theatre, wishing that it had been done by Verrio instead of Streater. James himself was not particularly popular in Oxford, or elsewhere for that matter. In September 1687 he came to Oxford; St Giles' was laid with gravel for the occasion. As James approached it began to rain, and soon the gravel turned to mud. Notwithstanding, tapestries were hung from upstairs windows, there was music, and speeches, and claret running from the conduit on Carfax. The King was noted to have on an old French hat 'not worth a groat', but he stayed at Christ Church where a Roman Catholic chapel had been erected in Canterbury Quad specially for him. While in Oxford, he touched for the King's Evil. The result is not recorded.

An unsuccessful interview with the dons of Magdalen, however, has come down to us. It was, according to James, a 'stubborn, turbulent college', and more trouble was to come when he decided to evict some of the Fellows.

Further visits took place, to the Bodleian and the Divinity School, where James attended a banquet in Selden End, where three hot dishes and twenty-eight cold ones were served, followed by fruit and sweetmeats. James remains in Oxford in statue form, at University College, dressed in a toga; nearby is his daughter, Anne, who replaced King Alfred there in 1700!

James's rival and successor, William of Orange, seems to have enjoyed his visit to the Theatre little better. After a banquet had been arranged there in his honour, at great expense and inconvenience, for the Bedels had to go up to London to buy goodies, William refused to taste so much as a mouthful, probably because he was afraid of being poisoned. Before Gown could help itself, Town rushed in and elbowed Gown aside, gobbling up everything that was going. Initials, and the date, 1688, are still visible outside the Theatre's west door.

Although the Hanoverians and Oxford took little notice of each other, George I did endow a chair of Modern History in 1724, and George II's queen, Caroline of Ansbach, surveys the hurly-burly of the city's main bus stop from her perch in Queen's cupola.

George III, his wife, and numerous offspring, spent quite a bit of time at Nuneham, not far away, and sometimes came as far as Oxford itself. In May 1785 they brought six of their children, and the following year heard a loyal address in the Theatre. The unfortunate George was attacked in the city by a crazed woman armed with an old fruit-knife, but escaped serious injury.

His son, George IV, on the other hand, fared much better while still Prince Regent, being given an honorary Doctorate of Civil Law at a ceremony in 1814, at which the allied commanders who had fought against Napoleon were also honoured. Beforehand a dinner was held in the Radcliffe Camera, the chief guests being the King of Prussia and the Czar of Russia, who also received honorary doctorates. Such a dinner was not repeated until 1988.

The Queen of George's brother and successor William IV, the 'quiet, plain-looking, spotty-faced' Adelaide, as a local clergyman so ungallantly described her, decided to stay at 'The Angel Hotel' in High Street, thus delivering quite a snub to Christ Church, which traditionally played host to royal personages. The Museum of Oxford recently paid £200 for a couple of the plates used at 'The Angel' on this occasion in 1835; they bear the royal couple's hastily added arms. Adelaide visited the Sheldonian Theatre and the Town Hall, where she listened to addresses. The account of her visit took up some five columns of *Jackson's Oxford Journal*.

Queen Victoria paid only the most fleeting of visits to Oxford to see the Prince of Wales, later Edward VII, who, although a member of Christ Church, actually lived at Frewin Hall in New Inn Hall Street, where his tutors came to visit him. Even so, Edward did not complete the course; this was not remarkable, for until Prince Charles's stay at Cambridge, royalty did not put themselves to the indignity of sitting examinations. Victoria made no secret of the fact that she hated the very name of Oxford, having been fired upon by an Edward Oxford while out riding in a carriage with Prince Albert shortly after their marriage. This did not stop her from founding chairs of Ecclesiastical History and Pastoral Theology in 1842, however.

Edward VIII was at Magdalen between 1921 and 1924, and George VI was once discovered, after he had temporarily gone missing, enjoying looking through the President of St John's stamp collection, in his lodgings. The King opened the New Bodleian, the foundation stone of which had been laid by his mother, Queen Mary. Embarrassingly, the silver key broke in the royal hand, but is still treasured by the Library.

Both the present Prince of Wales and Prince Edward went to Cambridge, but Charles was made an Oxford man by the conferral of an honorary Doctorate of Civil Law in 1983, while his Princess attended a degree ceremony incognito, in order to watch her brother, Viscount Althorp, receive his BA from Magdalen College in November 1986.

The second royal dinner held in the Radcliffe Camera, in July 1988, also featured Prince Charles. It was an unusually fine evening, and the 200 umbrellas which the Bodleian had ordered to protect the guests were not needed. Needless to say, the dinner was very impressive, with the doctors in their scarlet, flowers everywhere, and Charles himself in his DCL robe. Later, he was presented with a silver Bodleian reader's card.

Over the centuries, many royal persons have been awarded honorary doctorates, not only the British royal family, but those from all over the world, recent examples being the King of the Belgians, and the King and Queen of Spain.

BRITISH PRIME MINISTERS EDUCATED AT OXFORD

Name and Year of Office	College	Matriculated
Spencer Compton 1742–3	Trinity	1690
Henry Pelham 1743–54	Hart Hall	1710
George Grenville 1763–6	Christ Church	1730
William Pitt (the Elder) 1766–8	Trinity	1726
Lord North 1770–82	Trinity	1749
William Petty 1782	Christ Church	1755
William Cavendish-Bentinck 1783, 1807–9	Christ Church	1755
Henry Addington 1801–4	Brasenose	1774
Lord Grenville 1806–7	Christ Church	1776
Earl of Liverpool 1812–27	Christ Church	1787
George Canning 1827	Christ Church	1787
Sir Robert Peel 1834, 1841–6	Christ Church	1805
Edward Stanley, Earl of Derby 1852, 1858–9, 1866–8	Christ Church	1817
W. E. Gladstone 1868–74, 1880–85 1886, 1892–4	Christ Church	1828
Robert Cecil, Marquis of Salisbury 1885–6, 1886–92 1895–1902	Christ Church	1847
Earl of Rosebery 1894–5	Christ Church	1866
Herbert Henry Asquith 1908–15, 1915–16	Balliol	1870
Clement Attlee 1945–51	University	1901
Sir Anthony Eden 1955–7	Christ Church	1919
Harold Macmillan 1957–63	Balliol	1912

St Martin's Church, Carfax, *c*.1888

Carfax today

Coach and six on the frozen river, 1895

Punting on the Cherwell in Edwardian days

View from the Sheldonian over Broad Street

Morris dancing on St John's College Parvis

Turf Tavern, Bath Place

Sir Alec Douglas-Home 1963–4	Christ Church	1922
Harold Wilson 1964–70, 1974–6	Jesus	1934
Edward Heath 1970–74	Balliol	1935
Margaret Thatcher 1979–	Somerville	1943

OLD BOYS AND GIRLS

Name	*College*
Adams, Thomas	Brasenose
Alexander of Tunis, Earl	Trinity
Amis, Kingsley	St John's
Archer, Jeffrey	Brasenose
Arnold, Matthew	Balliol and Oriel
Attlee, Clement	University
Auden, W.H.	Christ Church
Bannister, Roger	Exeter and Pembroke
Beecham, Thomas	Wadham
Beerbohm, Max	Merton
Belloc, Hilaire	Balliol
Bentham, Jeremy	Queen's
Betjeman, John	Magdalen
Bridges, Robert	Corpus Christi
Buchan, John	Brasenose
Burton, Richard	Exeter
Campion, Edmund	St John's
Carroll, Lewis	Christ Church
Churchill, Lord Randolph	Merton
Day, Robin	St Edmund Hall
Day Lewis, C.	Wadham
Donne, John	Hart Hall
Douglas-Home, Alec	Christ Church
Eden, Anthony	Christ Church
Edward, the Black Prince	Queen's
Edward VII	Christ Church
Edward VIII	Magdalen
Eliot, T.S.	Merton
Evelyn, John	Balliol
Florey, Howard	Magdalen and Queen's
Fox, Charles James	Hertford
Fraser, Lady Antonia	Lady Margaret Hall

Fulbright, James	Pembroke
Galsworthy, John	New College
Gandhi, Indira	Somerville
Gibbon, Edward	Magdalen
Gladstone, W.E.	Christ Church
Golding, William	Balliol
Graves, Robert	St John's
Greene, Graham	Balliol
Grey, Earl	Balliol
Guthrie, Sir Tyrone	St John's
Haig, Field Marshal	Brasenose
Halley, Edmund	Queen's
Hampden, John	Magdalen
Heath, Edward	Balliol
Hemery, David	St Catherine's
Henry V	Queen's
Hobbes, Thomas	Hertford (Magdalen Hall)
Hopkins, Gerard Manley	Balliol
Housman, A.E.	St John's
Hunter, John	St Mary's (Oriel)
Huxley, Aldous	Balliol
Huxley, Julian	Balliol
Jenkins, Roy	Balliol
Johnson, Samuel	Pembroke
Juxon, William	St John's
Keble, John	Corpus Christi and Oriel
Laud, William	St John's
Lawrence, T.E.	Jesus and All Souls
Lewis, C.S.	University and Magdalen
Locke, John	Christ Church
Mackenzie, Sir Compton	Magdalen
MacNeice, Louis	Merton
Macmillan, Harold	Balliol
Moore, Dudley	Magdalen
More, Sir Thomas	St Mary Hall (Oriel)
Morris, William	Exeter
Murdoch, Iris	Somerville
Nash, 'Beau'	Jesus
Newman, John	Trinity and Oriel
North, Lord	Trinity
Olav of Norway, King	Balliol
Osler, Sir William	Christ Church
Pearson, Lester	St John's
Peel, Robert	Christ Church
Penn, William	Christ Church

Pitt, William (the Elder)	Trinity
Raleigh, Sir Walter	Oriel
Rantzen, Esther	Somerville
Rattigan, Terence	Trinity
Renault, Mary	St Hugh's
Rhodes, Cecil	Oriel
Rusk, Dean	St John's
Ruskin, John	Christ Church
Salisbury, Lord	Christ Church
Sayers, Dorothy L.	Somerville
Shaftesbury, Lord	Christ Church
Shelley, Percy Bysshe	University
Sidney, Sir Philip	Christ Church
Smith, Adam	Balliol
Smithson, James	Pembroke
Swift, Jonathan	Hertford
Swinburne, Algernon	Balliol
Thatcher, Margaret	Somerville
Tolkien, J.R.R.	Exeter, Pembroke and Merton
Tyndale, William	Hertford
Vaughan, Henry	Jesus
Walton, William	Christ Church
Waugh, Evelyn	Hertford
Wesley, Charles	Christ Church
Wesley, John	Lincoln and Christ Church
Wilde, Oscar	Magdalen
Wilson, Harold	Jesus and University
Wolsey, Thomas	Magdalen
Wren, Christopher	Wadham and All Souls
Wycliffe, John	Balliol

Note: when more than one college appears after a person's name, the first is the undergraduate college, the following where a fellowship has been held, or postgraduate qualifications obtained.

8 THE GHOSTS OF OXFORD

Oxford is a very haunted city, that much is sure. Nobody would be surprised to learn that the colleges and other ancient buildings are host to innumerable ghostly visitors, nameless or otherwise. Moreover, the city would appear to have a long history of hauntings, as the seventeenth-century example from Merton College shows. Sightings are a venerable institution in their own right, and no tourist attraction to be brought out and dusted down in the spring, only to be confined to moth-balls again as winter approaches.

As long ago as 1889, the Society for Psychical Research sent out questionnaires to 17,000 volunteers in order to compile a 'Census of Hallucinations'. Almost one person in ten, of the sample who were invited to answer the questions, replied that they had indeed had some sort of experience which they were unable to explain. The final results showed, without doubt, that sightings were more common in Oxford than anywhere else.

Apart from a number of first-hand accounts sent in as a response to such surveys or to newspapers running articles on such matters, there exists a whole range of stories. Some, like that of Prince Rupert and his troopers, have a sound basis in historical fact, some, like the Playhouse apparition are based on supposition, while a third category consists of those stories which are obviously fictional but fun, and have been passed on along with genuine reports.

As an example of fanciful tales one might mention how, at the stroke of midnight, the New College gargoyles slither along New College Lane and into the Broad, where they proceed to dance with the Proctors outside the Clarendon Building. As there are only two Proctors and dozens of carvings, either the Senior Members have to work exceeding hard to avoid jealousy, or there must be a large number of wallflowers at the dance!

Oxford is eminently well-suited for the more conventional type of haunting for it is rich in some fifty acres of churchyard and cemetery. Small wonder that Jeremy Bentham, when an undergraduate at the Queen's College, feared to look out from his window across Queen's Lane, to the graveyard of St Peter in the East. Now Bentham himself has gone to join the spirits in the Other World, but so far no one has claimed to have seen him since.

By no means all of the Oxford experiences, however, are of the classical, medieval style, although there is a good assortment of variously coloured figures, mainly of the black, white, or grey, variety, in the colleges. Not surprisingly, there are also a few stylish and aristocratic ghosts, like that of the first Duke of Marlborough, who drives coach and horses along the Woodstock Road, each New Year's Eve. Although he has not been reported in recent years, he is only what one might expect in the home of the world's leading university.

All Souls College, dedicated to the souls of the 'faithful departed', who lost their lives in the Hundred Years War against France, has little more than a black monk who flits along to the chapel door; the Divinity School once housed a little pot-boy, who carried a tray full of tankards, but ceased to appear when an elderly employee left: Brasenose Lane was the scene of the extraction of a gambling and blaspheming undergraduate, through his study window, by Old Nick himself; St Giles' churchyard is haunted by an elegant Edwardian lady who crosses over the Woodstock Road and makes for Little Clarendon Street, opposite. These stories have little substance, but others form part of the centuries-old folk-lore of Oxford, and should be told in more detail.

MERTON COLLEGE

As befits one of the oldest and most attractive of colleges, Merton appears to be one of the most haunted.

A very old ghost indeed is said to walk the Old Library, that of

Duns Scotus (1266–1308) the theologian, who has for company that great benefactor of the University, Sir Thomas Bodley. Other stories heard from time to time concern a certain room which could never be slept in, and which was made into a part of the library.

A younger, and more recent, ghost which is occasionally seen in the college is that of an earnest young undergraduate who is dressed in clothes which date him from about the time of the Great War. He has a pink and scrubbed aspect, a short-back-and-sides haircut, and carries a notebook.

Merton's own personal historian, Anthony à Wood, who was born and also died at Postmasters' Hall, opposite the college, had himself a ghost story to relate. This one manifested itself in 1664:

In the month of Jan. my friend Mr. R.L. told me, as he was cutting up a calf's head on a Sunday morning, about 8 of the clock in his study, his dore stodd so much open that he might thrust his fist through, and hearing a russelling in his chamber, looked through that open space of his doore, and saw the appearance of a beautifull yong man with long flaxen haire to his middle and a silke studying gowne on: and going to his study doore and oping it asked 'Who is there, Sir John?' (meaning Sir John Hales who was his opposite neighbour) and going out into his chamber and seeing noe body, looked in his other study and none there either. Then he went to his chamber doore, and that was shut and lached and could not be opened and shut without noise. And opeing the doore Sir John Hales came out of his owne, who (i.e. R.L.) asked him wether he was in his chamber, who (i.e. J.H.) answered faithfully that he was not. Whereupon he took this to be an appearance.

ST JOHN'S COLLEGE

An early President of the College, Archbishop Laud, was beheaded in 1645, and first buried in the church of All Hallowes, Barking. Afterwards, however, his body was brought to Oxford to be buried in the chapel of his old college. The corpse was met by an advance party from the University at Wheatley, and taken first to St Mary the Virgin Church, and then on to St John's where he was finally 'inclosed in a wooden coffin, in a littel vault at the upper end of the chancell between the founder's (tomb) and Archbishop Juxon's. The next day they hung up seven streamers.' So says Anthony à Wood.

In spite of all this activity, the Archbishop is said to extricate himself periodically from his 'littel vault' and take himself along to the Library which bears his name, there to enact one of Oxford's best-known and least authenticated hauntings.

Few Oxford children have not heard about how Laud, headless, of course, arrives to play bowls with the equally headless Charles I. These gentlemen use the entire length of the Library floor as a bowling alley, and their own severed heads as bowls!

Unfortunately, there is no reliable or even recent account of this haunting to give us details of how this game is achieved. The only detail which is certain is that this sporting pair play along the Library floor at its former level, the boards having being altered over the centuries.

EXETER COLLEGE

The only remains of the original college buildings are in the old gatetower which dates from 1432. Known as Palmer's Tower, it was cleaned and restored in the late 1960s. This disturbance may have rid the college of one of its ghosts.

This was the somewhat distressing spectacle of a headless man who would throw himself from the top of the tower, no doubt reacting some long-forgotten tragedy.

Another strange haunting took place in Exeter, on no. 6 staircase. The 'victim' was Dr Thomas Wood, then an undergraduate, later a composer and broadcaster. On 31 October 1916 Dr Wood was just about to leave his rooms at the top of the staircase, when he was stopped in his tracks by a figure in his doorway. The light was already turned out, but he could see that:

A man was standing right up against me, with the narrow band of light under Sharp's door shining through his body, and he had no head. Words won't come fast enough. Buff coat; yellow slashings; black gown;

one hand up as though he were going to knock; the pinpoint of Sharp's
keyhole where his heart should be, and where his face should be …
nothing. He stood still while I could have counted … one, two, three,
four, and my hair bristled. Then he went – puff – out like a candle.

Needless to say, a search was carried out immediately, but
nothing at all untoward discovered. The next day, though,
Wood heard from his tutor how, the morning of his experience,
work had started on clearing out junk from below no. 6 staircase.
Most of it had been cleared by the evening and during the course
of the work the labourers had come across a statue.

It was of a man in seventeenth-century dress, and, although it
was quite battered, it was of definite historical interest. At his
tutor's invitation, Wood went down to the basement to look at
it, and found it to be a small figure of a man kneeling at prayer.

He was wearing his gown and a tunic that had slashed sleeves edged
with lace round the wrists. Faint traces of colour were left: brown. He
had no head. My hair bristles for the second time. I had seen the
original of this battered piece of marble. He came to knock on my door
last night.

Further investigation showed that the statue was identical to
that on a certain monument, one erected to John Crocker, a
gentleman-commoner from Devon who had been a member of
Exeter College, and had died on 29 April 1629.

It seems certain that the statue had been hidden away in the
basement under no. 6 staircase when the old Chapel was
replaced by the present Victorian one. Why though, had John
Crocker waited until 1916 to show himself, unless it was the fact
that his statue had been rediscovered?

Why did he choose to go up five flights of stairs to visit Dr
Wood in particular?

Whatever the reason, he has been locked away again behind
the massive Chapel doors in case he takes it into his head to
frighten any more Hallowe'en revellers in years to come.

JESUS COLLEGE

A 'living ghost' story was told by a Mr P.-J., who had rooms
right at the top of no. 1 staircase, in the First Quad. The year
was 1910, and the narrator was entertaining a friend, also a
member of the College.

Around midnight, during a break in the conversation, the
two students made their way over to the window, and stood
looking down at the quad, which was bathed in moonlight.
There they caught sight of their tutor, a Mr J., who was strolling
up and down, between Hall and Chapel, apparently enjoying
the night air before turning in.

After watching for a few minutes, the friends decided to pop
downstairs and follow Mr J., walking behind him as he patrolled.
They scuttled down the staircase, and hid themselves in a dark
porch. As the tutor executed a smart about-turn, they then
slipped out of the darkness and marched along behind him.

Not content with this, they then proceeded to whistle Mr J.'s
favourite hymn, 'All Through the Night', Jesus being the
Welshman's College. To their surprise and disappointment, he
took not the slightest bit of notice, and continued to stroll as if
he had not heard them.

After following him for a minute or two, they began to narrow
the distance between themselves and the tutor, who had
reached the end of the pavement. Just as he should have swung
round to face his students, he kept on walking – straight through
the six-foot-thick wall of Jesus Hall.

The friends stopped dead, and stared. Then they rushed over
to the place where the tutor had vanished into the masonry.
Incredulously they hunted around in the thick and knotted ivy
there, but of course found nothing.

In 1968, Mr P.-J., then aged 81, remembered every detail of
the incident:

> It was frightening and inexplicable. We were certain when we first saw
> the figure from my upstairs room that it was Mr J. We would not have
> rushed down to play this prank on him had we not been certain that it
> was our tutor ... We could see his white tie which was popular with
> non-conformist Welsh clergymen of the time, and every feature of his

face was visible. When we looked in the ivy when he had disappeared, we were both scared stiff and beat a retreat back up to my room. To this day no rational explanation has ever occurred to me.

The following day, the undergraduates set about ascertaining Mr J.'s whereabouts on the previous night, and found out that he had been staying with relatives at Wolvercote, several miles away.

MAGDALEN COLLEGE

During Trinity Term, 1968, a second-year student at Magdalen arose early one Sunday morning in order to write an essay. About 5.45, before even the deer in Magdalen Grove were awake, he left his room and walked along under the colonnaded arches of the New Building, noticing that the grass was still covered with dew.

He then glanced in the direction of the Cloisters, and caught sight of a black shape. This seemed to be heading in his direction, and, as it came nearer, he was able to see it better. It proved to be the silhouette of a headless figure, dressed in some kind of robe. He told the press:

It was walking in a straight line towards staircase 3, the next one to mine. Its clothes did not move as it came across the lawn, and it made no sound at all. There were no ordinary walking movements, even when it mounted the three steps into the Colonnade it appeared to glide rather than walk and still there was no ordinary swirling of the robe: it remained fixed. As it drew level with me in the Colonnade, I stared hard at the figure and where its head should have been I could only see the wooden door twenty yards further on at the end of the arches.

Even on the stone pavement of the Colonnade, there was no sound of movement or footsteps. As the figure approached the entrance to staircase 3, and came into a stronger light, it simply vanished from view. I never expected to see a ghost: I always thought that ghosts were white and made horrible noises. This one was black and silent and its limbs appeared not to move as it glided along.

I have never thought up a rational explanation even though I've often tried; the apparition defied the rational faculties.

What this student did not know at the time that he saw the ghost, was that a few weeks previously a first-year historian was making his way across the same lawn, between 11 p.m. and midnight, when he chanced to look across to his left. There he caught sight of:

A black silhouette keeping pace with me exactly as I walked towards the Colonnade. The figure kept pace exactly with me and I kept glancing to my left to look at it. There was no sound of footsteps. We went up the few steps under the arches together; it was about ten yards away. When I looked to my left after passing under the arch and into the Colonnade, I expected to see it still keeping pace with me, but it had disappeared completely.

The two undergraduates had not spoken to each other about their experience, and it was not until an investigation was carried out by a magazine that they found out that they had both seen an identical black figure, which had disappeared at exactly the same place in Magdalen Colonnade.

TRINITY COLLEGE

The history of the haunting of Trinity Chapel goes back to the 1950s, if not before. In 1966, the organ was rebuilt, and a special service held to celebrate the event. This service was well attended, but, after the first hymn, a weird wailing sound was heard to come from the fine new organ.

At the first opportunity, the Dean crept round to investigate. Imagine his horror when he found the organist slumped over the organ console, where he had collapsed following a fatal heart attack. The tragedy fed rumours that some evil ghost might be at large in Trinity Chapel.

A more verifiable experience was that of the Verger, who, one sunny morning in 1959, went to unlock the Chapel door, as was his custom. As he was dusting the pews, something drew his attention, and made him look to his right. When he did so, he saw a lady standing about ten feet away from him. She was dressed entirely in black, and was smiling at him. Here is his own account of what he saw:

> There was nothing at all ghostly about the figure; at first I thought it was a real person, but as I looked I realised that it couldn't be – I had just unlocked the Chapel doors. Her body was simply black and it was her face which I gazed at. It was beautiful and smiling and I could see every detail. We both stood still and I looked at her for about a minute and all the time she smiled. I started to move a pace or two nearer and looked down at the first step of the pews, taking my eyes off her for a second. When I looked up again there was nothing but the empty Chapel.
>
> I was overcome by the experience and, as I calmed down, I was aware of the nagging feeling that I half-recognised the figure. Although it did not look like anyone I had ever known, I recognised its features and manner in some odd way.
>
> When I got back to my house I looked on the mantel-piece at the photograph of my dead mother and I suddenly realised who the figure was.

WADHAM COLLEGE

One of the college legends is that a white monk walks from the doorway leading into the Chapel, across the Front Quad, up the steps into Hall, and then along to the High Table where he vanishes.

In the winter of 1964, Wadham's Head Porter, Mr A.R. was doing his usual security check just before midnight, and had just left the Hall. He was making for staircase no. 4 when:

> Some instinct made me turn round, and look towards the big double doors of the Chapel. There, standing in front of me, was a white figure looking at me. It was robed and seemed to be wearing a cowl. It was either a priest or a woman. It was definitely a human figure although a little cloudy. I suppose it was about six foot tall, and appeared to be looking my way. I was not afraid at all and moved on to staircase 4 where I looked round again to find that the figure was gone. I was not

tired at all because I hadn't been working during the day, and I
certainly wasn't expecting to see a ghost.

In the following June, Mr C., a scout at Wadham, was clearing
away after late dinner at High Table. The time was about 11.30
p.m., and there were three scouts in Hall. Just as he was leaving,
Mr C. turned, and, as if on impulse, glanced across to a grey
figure, robed and cowled, standing near the fireplace.

> I thought I was seeing things until I looked again. It was definitely a
> human figure, and the other scouts saw it too. It was about six feet tall,
> and looked like a priest. After a few seconds the figure vanished and I
> was staring into the empty Hall. I heard footsteps and I beat it quickly
> out of the Hall. If I saw it again I'd stick around and study it. I've been
> here nine years and I've never heard of a ghost in Wadham before.

A third account was given by a scout on staircase 15, Mr E.W.,
who saw precisely the same figure, in the same place, and whose
description tallies exactly with that of Mr C.'s ghost.

Yet another report was given by Wadham's Head Steward, Mr
M.H., who, when he had his experience of the figure in the
1960s, had been at the College for more than twenty years. He
explained:

> I have been in my office quite late at night on many occasions, and
> heard footsteps in the Hall directly above my office. The footsteps have
> walked down the Hall, but I've never heard them going back. Many
> times I've dashed up there only to find the Hall deserted. I've never
> seen the ghost. The footsteps stop directly above my room.

Mr H.'s room was situated exactly below where at least four
people have actually seen the ghostly monk, and, in addition to
Mr H.'s testimony, his colleague, the Head Chef, has also heard
the footsteps while the two men were in the Head Steward's
office, late at night.

NEW COLLEGE

The main entrance to the college is down New College Lane, a
medieval thoroughfare described by Max Beerbohm as a 'grim
ravine', but loved by others for its remoteness.

The lane itself is said to be haunted, some say by a spectral coach and horses which tear along its length between Catte Street and the High, while others have it that the ghostly hoofbeats belong to a troop of Prince Rupert's cavalry, on their way in the dead of night to reinact the ambushing of a Parliamentarian pay-train en route for London. It was such a skirmish which led to the fatality of John Hampden on Chalgrove Field, not many miles away, and maybe it is these very troops who killed him.

The lovely College Chapel, one of the finest in Oxford, would also seem to be haunted. One evening in 1962, a College Fellow, a lecturer in music, was alone there tidying up after a late rehearsal. Being an organist, Dr D.L. was quite accustomed to be alone in churches and chapels in the dark, and was less nervous than most people would have been at the prospect.

After clearing away some books, he turned off the lights, and was making his way towards the door at the far end, which was in darkness. Suddenly something told him to turn round, and, when he did so, he saw, from a range of less than five feet away, a man's white face above the Warden's stall.

'It was not a blur of light,' said Dr L., 'but a definite face, with all normal features; the body must have been dark because it was not visible in the pitch darkness of the Chapel. I assumed it was in academic or priestly dress. I turned away and walked on for a few paces. Then I realised what I had seen, and I ran all the way out of the Chapel. I was terrified, and since that time I have never stayed alone in the Chapel after dark.

Some of the College members have tried to persuade me that what I saw was the ghost of Warden Spooner, whose description tallied with what I saw. I do not know who it was, and I have no rational explanation for it.'

Dr W.A. Spooner, originator of many spoonerisms, was Warden from 1903 to 1924, and the 'white face' which Dr L. described may be relevant, for Dr Spooner was an albino.

THE UNIVERSITY CHURCH OF ST MARY THE VIRGIN

On a marble slab set into the floor, not far from the sanctuary steps, one may read that 'in a vault of brick, at the upper end of the quire of this church' lie the remains of Amy Robsart.

The unfortunate Amy was wife to Lord Robert Dudley, afterwards Earl of Leicester, Chancellor of the University, and favourite of Elizabeth I. In 1560, with her husband well in the Queen's good books, and, some say, even a possible suitor for her hand, had he been free to marry, Amy was the reputed victim of a poison attempt, while staying at Cumnor Hall, a few miles from Oxford.

The plot failed, but Anthony Foster, the owner of the Hall, and one of her husband's servants, sent all her servants off to Abingdon Fair for the day. When they returned, they found Amy lying at the foot of a flight of stairs, with her neck broken. Even these simple folk asked themselves why, if their mistress intended to do away with herself, were there marks of severe bruising round her neck, and her hood was neatly arranged on her head?

Certainly Amy was buried very hurriedly before the coroner had even had a chance to give his verdict. Amy's father, Sir John Robsart, arrived posthaste from Norfolk, and demanded that she be exhumed, pending an investigation. Before this could be done, however, her lord intervened, and, with a great show of grief, had Amy reburied in St Mary's on Sunday 22 September 1560 'with great pomp and solemnity'. Before this, Amy had lain in state at Gloucester Hall, now part of Worcester College.

Amy is said to haunt the Junior Common Room of Worcester, which is where her body lay that night. She is also said to have been very active at Cumnor Hall, so much so that it was abandoned and allowed to decay, last century.

Not deterred, she persisted in haunting Cornbury Park, not far from Charlbury. The records of her appearances there date from immediately after her death. Indeed, she materialized in front of the startled Leicester to inform him that, within ten days, he too would be in the same condition that she was now in. Whether from shock or existing natural causes, he obediently gave up the ghost within the stated time.

The Cornbury haunting continued to impress the locals, even to this day, so that if anyone meets Amy in the Park, it is said he or she would do well to prepare to meet their Maker!

Although, as far as is known, St Mary's itself is not haunted, it is the burial-place of a second Oxford ghost, one Prudence Burcote, a seventeenth-century serving-maid. Prudence lived and worked in a house nearly opposite the church, in Magpie Lane. It now belongs to Barclay's Bank, where Prue is well known, if only by repute.

Her presence has often been sensed by people who have that gift, and the bank staff have often heard inexplicable 'noises off' in the building.

Indeed, Prudence has actually been spotted on several occasions, by those living in and around Magpie Lane. She appears quite openly, in broad daylight, dressed in the costume of a Puritan maid-servant of the mid-seventeenth century, near the doorway of 'her' house. She is also known to the residents of nearby Merton Street, where she takes a stroll when she feels so inclined.

A check with the burial register of St Mary's church showed that a Prudence Burcote was indeed buried in 1643, the time when Oxford was the Royalist capital. Unfortunately, there are no further details, such as age or marital status, so we are left with the legend that she killed herself after being jilted by her Cavalier lover. More likely she died of the proverbial broken heart, and was thus able to be buried in consecrated ground in St Mary's churchyard.

THE PLAYHOUSE

A well-authenticated account of the Playhouse apparition dates from April 1978, and appeared in the local press. The sighting was reported by Mrs. F.D., a cleaner, who was collecting her mop and bucket from the basement, at 8.30 one morning.

A 'white lady' floated suddenly and alarmingly through a basement wall, the basement being a cellar-like structure, which is a good deal older than the theatre itself, which only dates from the 1930s. The lady then drifted past the startled Mrs D., only to disappear once again through the brickwork of the opposite wall.

This was not the first time that such a thing had happened, and so the staff of the Playhouse were stimulated into doing some research into the history of the building and its site. They discovered that the theatre stands on ground once occupied by a Carmelite monastery. These White Friars wore a cloak of that colour which formed part of their habit.

Mrs D. particularly mentioned the ghost's veil in her description of the white lady, and, although she believed the apparition to be that of a woman, it is possible that, in her state of shock, she assumed the figure to be clad in female attire rather than a cloak or robe.

The Playhouse staff also discovered that, when the present building was constructed in 1938, no less than fifteen medieval skulls were found, suggesting that the Carmelite theory was indeed correct, and that a burial-ground had been disturbed.

Nowadays the Playhouse is only open for the occasional production, leaving the white lady free to wander at will.

THE CASTLE AREA

A good example of a haunting which has passed into folklore is the case of the 'Maiden Kendalls', three unmarried sisters who lived in the parish of St Thomas's in the later Stuart period, and endowed charities there.

The best-documented sister is Anne, who, like her royal namesake, died in 1714. She left a considerable amount of money to the parish according to the terms of her will.

According to Oxford tradition, the Kendall sisters continued to appear on Quarter Days, doling out largesse to the deserving poor of the area, recognizable, as in life, by their grey silk dresses.

Unsocially-minded persons made attempts to exorcize them, but to no avail, despite the attentions of several local clergymen. The 'Maidens' insisted on carrying on the good work until no fewer than thirteen bishops intervened. Maybe the ladies scorned mere clergymen, their long association with the church having turned them into snobs.

Many Oxonians, however, remain unconvinced that even the bishops had been successful, and stories continue to circulate about a strange-looking lady in grey who frightens schoolchildren by vanishing if she is spoken to, and of three sisters who patrol a bridge in the vicinity of Oxford Castle.

PORT MEADOW

The meadow was used as an airfield during the last war, and a plaque at the north end, on the main road from Wolvercote to Godstow, commemorates two early airmen who lost their lives near the spot.

A worker at Lucy's Iron Foundry in Walton Well Road, just at the approach to the meadow, had a strange experience there a few years ago. He was walking along the road, just near the railway bridge, when he met another man coming in the opposite direction. He did not take much notice of the stranger as they passed, except to notice that he was wearing a flying-suit, something which struck him as a little unusual. As he turned round for a second look, the aviator disappeared completely.

In the summer of 1971, a party of lecturers and students were having a barbecue on the meadow, just opposite the Perch at Binsey. There was nothing remotely eerie about the place that they had chosen, and the atmosphere was cheerful and relaxed. They made a huge bonfire and cooked sausages and jacket potatoes. There was plenty of food and drink, but nothing stronger than lager, and certainly no drugs handed round. It was a beautiful night, and they could see right across to the Perch, a distance of several hundred yards, and watch the comings and goings of its customers.

Well after closing time, a figure became visible on the far bank. It gave the impression of suddenly being there, without actually moving into position. Gradually, everyone, lecturers and students alike, had noticed it, but, at first, no one said anything. Then it started to move along, against a hedge. They could make out no up-and-down motion, indeed its progress was remarkably even. Its appearance gave the watchers no indication of its sex, or even of any light, or dark areas to suggest a face, hair, or clothing.

It was just a uniformly grey figure, an outline, with no features or limbs, only head and shoulders defined. What was outstanding, however, was its height, which must have been about eight foot when compared with the pub customers who had been visible earlier in the evening at a similar distance. This estimate was verified by comparing it with an obliging cow which happened to amble along at the same time.

The figure made its stately way along, with everyone now watching intently. The students started to describe to each other what they could see, and, without exception, their accounts coincided. It was not at all frightening, only fascinating.

They had been studying Hamlet, and one of the party called out, 'I'll cross it though it blast me!', at the same time holding out his arms in the shape of a cross.

At this, the visitor looked as surprised as anything faceless can look, and stopped dead in its tracks. There it remained for several seconds, while it gave the distinct impression of staring, while it decided what to do next. Finally, it moved off again, then started to disintegrate. After fifteen seconds or so there was no trace of it to be seen. The students continued to stare. Someone thought to look at the time; it was 12.05 in the morning.

A couple of days later one of them said, 'I wonder what the date was when we had the barbecue, and if it's the anniversary of anything.' When they worked it out, they realized that it was 23/24 June: Midsummer's Eve.

GODSTOW

Two girls who had brought their caravan onto Port Meadow and parked it in the grounds of the ruined nunnery there, invited a local doctor and his daughter to stay up on watch with them during the hot July night. The girls had been troubled by nocturnal noises which suggested that a group of people had been walking round their caravan. This had happened on several nights, but it did not happen the night that the visitors were there. The girls stayed awake on guard, with a male undergraduate friend to keep them company.

About four in the morning, the doctor's daughter woke him to say that the other three were standing just by the chapel door of the nunnery, engrossed by something or somebody inside the ruined building.

They mentioned nothing about this, though, when they

returned to the caravan. One of the girls did ask the doctor if he happened to know whereabouts the altar would have stood. At length she revealed that, while the three of them had kept their vigil, a light had suddenly appeared among the ruins. On looking more closely, they were able to see a priest who was celebrating Mass in the chapel.

In a statement to a local paper, the doctor quoted his informant as saying: 'The altar lights were two enormous candles, the vestments were very beautiful, and the early morning sun was shining through three lancet windows, two of which have long since been bricked up.'

The three young people were not in the least scared, and stayed watching until the Mass vision faded away as suddenly as it had come.

At a later date the doctor took the opportunity of questioning the undergraduate closely about what he had seen, and his description matched that of the girl in every way.

A report in the *Oxford Mail* of August 1966, told of how a couple of friends from Reading were staying in a cabin-cruiser which one of them owned, and which was moored on the river bank at Godstow.

About 11 o'clock one night they were strolling along the towpath when they chanced upon not one ghost, but two. One took the form of a lady in a long, flowing gown. She kept bending down as if she were trying to pick up some invisible object on the ground. The second was a male figure which wore a hat with a turned-down brim, and a short jacket. What was even stranger about him was the fact that he tapered away, just below the knees.

The friends stood and watched for about ten minutes, and, although the evening was dark and misty, the apparitions appeared to be luminous in some way, for they would vanish for a few seconds and then reappear, as if they were being switched on and off by some mysterious force.

At last the watchers could bear it no longer. They called out, 'Who are you? What do you want?' The only response to this was a sort of muttering. Neither man much cared to pursue the matter further, so they edged gingerly past the ghostly pair, and ran on to their boat. When they were safely aboard, they put on some cheerful music, in the hope of calming themselves down a little, and to bring themselves back to reality.

Not being local – one, in fact, came from Jamaica – they had never heard of Godstow's ghostly reputation, nor the fact that Fair Rosamund, mistress to Henry II, is said to haunt the place, as well as appearing at Blenheim Palace. It was not until they went into work that they were enlightened.

Two weeks later, while his West Indian friend was away for the weekend, the owner of the cabin-cruiser was treated to a repeat performance of the scene. This time the vision was less distinct than before, but he was still able to recognize the ghosts and their strange routine.

WOLVERCOTE

A rather creepy little tale is told concerning a certain vicar of Wolvercote, who, late one dark night in 1744, was making his way home from Oxford. Suddenly, his lantern went out, for no apparent reason.

As he stood there in the total darkness, wondering what had happened, he heard a child crying nearby. Then, just as suddenly as it had been extinguished, the lantern came back to life again. By its light he was able to make out a second lantern, sitting by the side of the road.

The vicar, reasoning that something unusual was afoot, and that he was expected to do something, decided to rush off and find a spade. Digging away at the spot illuminated by the strange lantern, he eventually came upon the skeleton of a child.

The kindly man took up the small collection of bones, and gave them Christian burial in his own churchyard.

Over the years a story has evolved to the effect that the crying child was one shot by the Royalist guard defending Godstow House, but whoever the child really is, he or she is certainly in good company on haunted Port Meadow.

HEADINGTON, BARTON

The area between Bayswater Road, Headington, and the A40 to

London, is an exceptionally well-haunted part of Oxford, and can almost rival Port Meadow in the variety and frequency of its apparitions, but the rest of this area is not far behind.

A large black dog is reported to patrol between Mathers Farm and the corner of Larkins Lane, in Old Headington, and accompanies walkers as far as Ashot (otherwise Ashlot) where it vanishes. Perhaps he is something to do with the horseman who gallops along the path to Beckley, only to disappear also. It is more likely, though, that he is a relative of the Black Shuck, the giant ghost-dog with eyes like coach-lamps, a legacy of our Scandinavian ancestors. Interestingly, Ashot is one of those ancient pathways along which the carrying of a corpse ensures a right-of-way.

The rider referred to above is a frequent and well-known visitor, and has been coming for years. His fame has spread as far as Australia, where his tale is told by someone who met him in 1979.

A sales representative was driving along the A40, near Barton Estate, when a phantom horseman suddenly emerged on a white horse, jumped over the hedge, and then vanished.

The first time that he saw the rider, he did not dare to tell anyone in case he was thought to be going mad, but when it happened a second time, some time later, he told his wife. After a third sighting, they were both extremely intrigued. Shortly afterwards, however, they emigrated to Australia, having had no chance to investigate.

Local residents, though, are quite used to the story of the ghostly rider; sometimes he is said to be dressed as a medieval knight, at others more like a Cavalier, so it is possible that there are not one but two phantom horsemen, sharing the one haunt.

Not surprisingly, the vicinity of the Crematorium is reputedly haunted. One ghost is popularly supposed to be that of the first woman to be cremated there, but in 1958 a man out walking his dog, experienced a sighting which was ascribed to a different source.

He was coming from the direction of Stanton St John when his collie froze in her tracks, then began to snarl and growl. The animal was trembling all over, and was stiff with terror as she stared fixedly ahead.

On following her stare, her owner also saw what was distressing the dog. A vague shape, misty, and palish-charcoal in colour, was moving slowly along and then crossed a stream. It was about five feet tall, and made its way across a bridge. As man and dog watched together, it disappeared while still travelling up the stream.

On making enquiries, the man later found out that a fatal accident had taken place at this spot, when a car had crashed on this bridge and ended up in the stream.

In the autumn of 1981 Wick Farm, Barton, came into the news as the haunt of Nellie (otherwise known as Nannie) Martin. The *Oxford Star* received a letter of enquiry as to the origins of her story, as the writer had seen what seemed to be a ghost about two fields away from the farm.

One of the most comprehensive of the accounts received, tells how Nellie, a servant girl at this remote house, gave birth to a baby, presumably illegitimate. One stormy winter night she ventured forth and drowned it in the Roman bath belonging to the farm. She then set off across the fields, only to sink into a bog near the farm buildings. Because of the wildness of the night, no one heard her cries for help, and, in her weakened condition, she quickly died of exposure.

Another version has it that she drowned the child, and then herself, while a third tells how the child's father murdered them both.

Soon after her death Nellie started to walk from Wick Farm to Stow Wood, and she has been sighted at the farm itself, as well as as far away as Elsfield. She has acquired a reputation for being a friendly and helpful phantom, for she chases away thieves intent on stealing apples, and opens gates for tired farmers.

Her costume has been described as being Elizabethan, and it is generally agreed that she is lovely to look at. Unfortunately, a drunken farmhand took the liberty of trying to kiss her, at which she started up and ran away, never to be seen again, having had more than enough of that sort of thing! If whatever the letter-writer saw was indeed Nellie, though, she may have plucked up courage to walk again after a long interval.

HEADINGTON HILL

In 1825 the new St Clement's church was constructed at the bottom of Headington Hill, just into the Marston Road. Although the £6,500 needed for its foundation was raised by subscription from such worthies as Keble, Pusey, Heber, and Sir Robert Peel, it was not a popular building, and was referred to unflatteringly as the 'Boiled Rabbit' by the locals.

Just before the outbreak of the First World War, a man was cycling to work at about 5.30 in the morning. Just as he was approaching the junction of Marston Road and St Clement's Street, he became aware of a white figure which was drifting in and out among the trees in Headington Hill Park. As he watched, leaning on his bike as if hypnotized, it began to glide over the stone wall of the Park. It then crossed the road and made towards St Clement's graveyard where it disappeared among the graves.

Headington Hill Hall lies at the top of Headington Hill, and is occupied by millionaire and football tycoon, Robert Maxwell.

When the Maxwell family moved into the Hall, they had a lot of trouble with the drains. The City Architect was called in, and he struggled bravely with the problem for eight long years, but all to no avail.

Finally he went to Mrs Maxwell to say that, sorry as he was, there was no more he could do to help, as the entire house was 'founded on that drain'. Furthermore, he declared, 'You'd have to be a ghost to get down there and clear them.'

Two days after that, the unfortunate architect hanged himself. On the very night that he committed suicide, the Hall drains righted themselves never to be troublesome again.

NORTHWAY ESTATE

Although the estate is of recent construction, not being started until the 1950s, an earlier occupant of the site is still interested in the land.

According to a young lady who used to live in a house which

backed on to a large field, with many trees and ditches, a radiant lady continues to walk around Northway.

On returning home one evening, the lady's attention was drawn across to the far side of the field where stood a lady with long, blond hair, wearing a glowing white dress, which could have been described as dazzling. The figure carried in her hands a large brown package in front of her, supporting it carefully with both hands. She walked straight towards the onlooker, but what was amazing about her progress was the fact that she was walking right through trees and ditches, and, although she seemed to be walking at only a moderate speed, the amount of ground which she covered was immense.

Within only a few seconds she was standing at the bottom of the garden, with only a wire mesh fence separating her from the watcher's garden. For a split second she hesitated, and then came on, straight through the fence, and onto the property.

The lady then went behind a willow tree in the garden, but, when the owner went over to investigate, she found nothing at all. As she had only a matter of seconds in which to make her getaway, the radiant lady could only have vanished, or else she would have been seen reappearing on the other side of the tree.

The owner of the garden afterwards moved away from North-way Estate, thus having no further chance to renew her acquaintanceship with the mysterious blonde.

IFFLEY

The village's main thoroughfare, Church Way, was the scene of a lighthearted haunting at some unspecified date in the past. The ghost itself has been described as wearing a large, soft hat, and being the owner of a wooden leg. It has been presumed to be that of a sailor, both from its attire, and from its lack of a leg.

It took to roaming round the village late at night, and would make such a clatter with its ghostly stump, that it became a confounded nuisance to one and all. When the inhabitants of Iffley had had enough of it, and could stand no more, they invited certain members of the local clergy to perform an exorcism in order to rid themselves of the prowler. However, these reverend gentlemen declined the invitation, for reasons best known to themselves.

Not deterred, the villagers accepted the offer of a down-and-out who claimed to have seen service with a naval chaplain, perhaps on the assumption that he would have had experience of wooden legs, ghostly or otherwise.

The evening before the confrontation was due, the self-appointed ghost-hunter was plied with Dutch courage, and, when the ghost arrived, the village champion lurched into action. His technique was disastrous.

He stood, vainly trying to keep his balance, in the middle of Church Way, waving a bicycle pump, and getting aggressive with the villagers themselves. He was much more of a menace than the poor old ghost, who could not help tapping his peg-leg, but had never been abusive or said a wrong word.

So unpleasant did the situation become that the police were called in, and carted the troublemaker away to Oxford, leaving the ghost to have the last laugh.

9 OXFORD TODAY

Selective Shopping; Oxford's Museums and Galleries; Music in
Oxford; Drama in Oxford; Eating and Drinking in Historical
Surroundings; The Oxford Year; Some Oxford Villages

This chapter is intended for those who, maybe because they
have already seen most of the colleges, do not particularly wish
to do so anyway, or have come to Oxford for a longer period of
time than the average visitor, are looking for something else to
do in the city and the surrounding area. It is hoped, therefore,
that an accurate picture will be built up of Oxford as a modern,
industrial, international city, with more to it than the
University and its colleges and institutions.

The break away from the dreaming spires and ivory towers
mould has, naturally enough, brought disadvantages. It cannot
be emphasized strongly enough, for example, that to bring a car
into the centre of Oxford is sheer folly. The one-way system, the
lack of parking facilities, and the volume of traffic in the narrow
streets, combine to make it difficult enough for the pedestrian,
without the added responsibility of watching the road, and
finding somewhere to leave the car.

Unless the visitor has contacts in Oxford, and a safe place to
leave his car and proceed on foot, he would be well advised to
make use of the excellent Park and Ride services, which offer
free parking with the purchase of a bus ticket into the centre.
Park and Ride services run north-south from Pear Tree to
Redbridge, at the end of the Abingdon Road, and east-west from
Thornhill on the London Road at Headington, to Seacourt, off
the Botley Road.

For those who are forced to bring a car, there is a multi-storey car-park in the Westgate Centre, and off-street parking in Broad Street and St Giles' with more car-parks in Gloucester Street and off St Clement's, just that bit further from the centre. Do not, however, think that you will be able to drive gently from college to college, stopping to admire the sights on the way.

WALKING TOURS

The Guild of Oxford Guides awards its Blue Badge only after a rigorous programme of study and training. There are other guides in Oxford, some of them perfectly competent, others fly-by-night, the latter usually being students in need of extra money for their holidays during the Long Vacation. Some take great pains to ensure that their information is correct, but others are concerned only with raising the necessary cash. The visitor is not likely to go far wrong if he joins a walking tour organized by the Guild, as its members are mostly professional or academic people, doing this exacting and tiring job because they enjoy it, and love Oxford, rather than for financial gain.

Everyday tours are conducted in English, although foreign language tours in the major European languages may be booked in advance. Tickets are on sale in the Tourist Information Centre, St Aldate's, with a maximum of twenty people to each tour. The meeting point is in the Town Hall, opposite the Centre. 1988/89 prices are £2.40 for an adult, and £1 for a child, and the tour lasts about two hours. The times at which they leave vary depending upon the time of year and demand; for up-to-date information, ring (0865) 726871.

Each tour will depend for its contents upon the particular group's requirements, which may vary according to age, interest, or nationality. For instance, party bookings made for visiting academics, scientists, gardening enthusiasts or architects will each have a different slant. In addition, there are special-subject tours, led by experts. At the moment these are on 'Alice' in Oxford; American Roots; the Civil War and the Seventeenth Century; Literary Figures, and Modern Architecture. Once again, enquiries to the Information Centre or on (0865) 726871.

SELECTIVE SHOPPING

Although Woolworth's have closed down their city-centre branch, and British Home Stores have not yet moved in, Oxford has the usual selection of chain-stores, plus Fenwick, now Lewis's, and Liberty. It is, however, the smaller and more individual shops which attract visitors to Oxford, in search of that unusual gift or distinctive souvenir, which somehow typifies the University city.

Academic Dress Makers

It is encouraging to know that Oxford's robes and gowns are still manufactured in the city, in businesses which have been in the same families for several generations. It is possible to buy any item of academic dress, from a white bow-tie to a complete Doctor of Divinity gown with scarf, but unless the item is to be worn frequently, most people prefer to hire.

The leading shops, Shepherd and Woodward in the High Street, who also own Walters' outfitters in Turl Street, Castells, in Broad Street, and Hall Brothers, also in the High Street (and proudly displaying the Prince of Wales feathers) display the items themselves, plus their charges for hire.

Even Oxford is subject to the trends of the twentieth century. The fur on hoods is now almost invariably fake, as a gesture of goodwill to both rabbits and conservationists, and the Doctor of Music's gorgeous gown, usually described as being of cerise and ivory silk, is today made of nylon. It remains a costly item, at well over £100, and the silk version is still available, at a much higher cost of course.

Of greater interest to visitors, and those who wish to give an Oxonian present to friends and relations overseas, is the wide range of clothing and accessories for sale in the academic dress shops. The most popular are tee shirts and sweat shirts with either the University or a college crest on them. Perhaps surprisingly, these shops offer such items at competitive prices, and carry a much wider selection than do the stalls which appear in Oxford's streets in the summer. Also for sale in the shops are sweaters, ties and tie-pins, cuff-links, key-rings, cloth badges, boater-ribbons in college colours, scarves and even miniature rugby balls, for the man who has everything.

Alice's Sheep Shop
83 St Aldate's

Nearly opposite Christ Church Memorial Gardens is a small, stone-built shop. It dates from the Middle Ages, but was remodelled in the seventeenth century. It derives its strange name from *Alice in Wonderland*, where the heroine goes into a similar shop to find it in the care of an elderly sheep, busy with her knitting.

The shop would have been familiar to both Lewis Carroll, who, as C.L. Dodgson, was a mathematics don at Christ Church, and to his small friend, Alice Liddell, daughter of the Dean. Alice would buy her barley-sugar in the Sheep Shop. Today, it sells gifts and souvenirs, most of which are 'Alice' memorabilia.

Laura Ashley
26–7 Cornmarket Street and 26 Ship Street

Laura Ashley shops are normally an attraction for shoppers, but this one in Oxford city centre must be unique. For nearly 130 years its owners, Zacharias's outfitters, were a household name in Oxford, but on the closure of 'Zac's' in 1983, the owners, Jesus College, began an outstanding programme of renovation.

The Cornmarket Street building was completely dismantled, then reconstructed, using as many of the original timbers as was practical. In all the structural timbers, no nails, screws, or glue were used, only pegs. A new frontage of English oak was inserted on the first floor, and may easily be seen from the street as it has been left its natural colour so that one may appreciate the blend of ancient and modern craftsmanship. This frontage contains modern replicas of the row of fifteenth-century oak window-frames, left unglazed, the glass being set back into the room.

Laura Ashley occupies the renovated shop, while Jesus College has student rooms on the third floor. The rear portion of the shop takes up what used to be an inn courtyard during the late Middle Ages, and, if one looks up and back from the ground floor, it is possible to see the good fourteenth-century jettying. What is now the upper sales floor would have had no ceiling, but have been open to the roof.

The Bodleian Library Proscholium

If planning a visit to the Divinity School, spare a few minutes to browse through the Bodleian shop, which is situated in the right-hand section of the entrance foyer, or Proscholium.

The majority of the stock is connected with the library's treasures, the more predictable post-cards, booklets, slides, posters and book-marks, but other items are much more original, such as the solid oak book-rest similar to those actually used in the reading-rooms, or the umbrellas with the Bodleian logo. These were ordered to protect guests walking across to the Radcliffe Camera, when Prince Charles came to dine there in August 1988. The evening being a fine one, the umbrellas were not needed, hence the sale. The post-cards and greetings-cards, showing anything from Anglo-Saxon ailments and their cures to a map of Tolkien's Middle Earth, will not be found elsewhere. All in all, the Proscholium is the place for unusual and reasonably priced Oxford gifts.

Bookshops

Hardly surprisingly, Oxford abounds in bookshops, from the general to the specialist, from international concerns to private enterprise on home premises where an appointment is necessary to view the stock. Twenty-three booksellers, from all over Oxford, have joined together to produce a booklet, *Antiquarian and Secondhand Bookdealers in Oxford*, which is obtainable free from any of those concerned.

The leading sellers of both new and used books are *Blackwell's*, of Broad Street, who also have a rare and antiquarian section at Fyfield Manor, near Abingdon. Blackwell's is one of Europe's largest booksellers, with over 200,000 titles on several floors. Under the same ownership are the Paperback Shop and the Art Shop, on the opposite side of Broad Street from the main shop, and the Music Shop, which also deals with concert tickets, just down the road in Holywell Street. The former Blackwell's Art Shop, between the main shop and the White Horse, is now devoted to maps and travel books.

Thornton's of Oxford, again in the Broad, opposite Balliol, is a long-established family concern, once famous for its cobwebby corners, original William Morris wallpaper, and its Victorian lavatory. Recently, however, it has been taken over and given a face-lift, which while destroying much of its atmosphere, must have done wonders for the staff!

A giant newcomer, *Dillon's*, is on the corner of Broad Street and Cornmarket, while *Waterfield's*, in Park End Street, not far from the railway station, offers four floors of second-hand and antiquarian stock.

There are numerous smaller, specialist shops, like the *Classics Bookshop*, near Queen's Lane, and *Sanders* of Oxford, at 104 High Street which is strong on prints and maps, as well as the second-hand bookshops in the Turl, stationers such as *W.H. Smith* in Cornmarket, and *Book Bargains* in St Ebbe's, which offers new books at remainder prices. Watch out, too, for book fairs held periodically at St Michael's church hall in Cornmarket, at the Polytechnic, and at the Randolph Hotel in Beaumont Street.

Frank Cooper's Marmalade Shop

84 High Street

In 1874, Mrs Sarah Cooper made seventy-six pounds of marmalade in her own home, using a recipe which had been in the family for years. Her husband, Frank, packaged up what was not needed for the family's own use, and sold it in his grocery shop, in the earthenware jars which have since become collectors' items. So popular was this venture, that the Coopers moved from their High Street shop to larger premises in Park End, Street, and finally to even larger ones in the Botley Road.

In 1919 Frank Cooper Ltd received the coveted Royal Warrant as Marmalade Manufacturers to Queen Alexandra; it was again awarded in 1938 by the Prince of Wales, in 1941 by George VI, and by our present Queen in 1955.

Besides being in world-wide demand, Cooper's marmalade went to the South Pole with Scott, and up Everest with Hilary and Tensing. Although Frank Cooper produce is now made in Redditch, the wheel has turned full circle for the original shop in High Street has re-opened, selling marmalade, preserves, mustard and other high-quality provisions, and it has become something of a tourist attraction once again.

The Covered Market
Between High Street and Market Street

On 27 February 1773, *Jackson's Oxford Journal* reported:

> On Tuesday last was laid the first stone of the four Houses to be erected in High Street, fronting our New Market in which there are to be three commodious Avenues opening thereto.
>
> This Market is to consist of four Ranges of Shops, the inner ones are secured from the weather by a lofty covered Way forming a Central Passage and those on each side encompassed by a colonnade.

Thus began one of Britain's oldest surviving covered markets, and one of the most interesting, too. Although the majority of its shops are butchers, fruiterers, and other purveyors of foodstuffs, their merchandise has something of Fortnum and Mason about it, consisting as it does of quails' eggs, kiwi fruit, octopus, venison, goat's cheese, French pastries, speciality teas and coffees, alligator steaks, and other such exotica.

Furthermore, there are florists, a pet shop, shoe-shops, a cobbler's, cafés, and woollen and fancy-goods emporia; in short, one may buy anything from budgies to bhajis. George's Café, once celebrated for its hearty breakfasts and dripping toast, has gone completely up-market and transformed itself into the bistro-like Beaton's, but Georgina's restaurant survives upstairs.

Gill's, the Ironmongers
128a High Street

While not claiming that their stock is in any way unique or aimed at the average visitor, Gill and Co. are the oldest ironmongers in the country, dating back to 1530. They have even produced a pamphlet which shows the family tree!

As ironmongers, Gill and Co. have a reputation locally for offering old-fashioned service, and for keeping a comprehensive stock which goes back long before metrication, and the fashion for buying everything in larger quantities than one needs.

Golden Cross Walk

Leading from Cornmarket Street into the Covered Market, Oxford's latest shopping attraction stands on a very old site.

Its history has been recorded since at least the mid-fourteenth century, when it was occupied by 'Gingiver's Inn', from about 1356 until 1388. Then it became 'The Cross Inn' in the fifteenth century, and, in 1764, 'The Golden Cross'. The eastern section was added last century. Originally the property consisted of four shops and an adjacent property, which was rented, all dating from the late twelfth century, and making up the inn. This was bought by William of Wykeham, founder of New College, in 1388, and was owned by the college until 1825, when it was sold for £2,550.

In one of the upstairs rooms, a series of fourteenth-century black and white drawings executed on plaster were found, hidden behind wallpaper. 'The Golden Cross' was recently converted into separate shops on its ground floor, after having been a steak house. It is now an exclusive shopping arcade, centred on the inn courtyard.

The more unusual shops are those selling teas and teapots of every conceivable type; herbal and traditional remedies, and speciality foodstuffs; hand-made chocolates; silk underwear; and, perhaps the most exclusive of all, the 'Oxford Collection' of high-quality gifts and souvenirs, most of which bear 'themes and designs connected with the University in general, and the Bodleian Library in particular.' These include playing cards, silk scarves, stationery, glass and ceramics, not to mention teddy bears sporting Oxford tee shirts.

Past Times

4 Turl Street

'Historical replicas and gifts that re-create the past', is how this enticing shop describes its stock. The times past range from prehistoric to the 1940s, and cover such cultures as those of Greece, Rome and Islam, as well as our own from Anglo-Saxon times onwards. Items for sale include records and cassettes, books and cards, jewellery, toys and games, and even garden statues of David and Venus!

OXFORD'S MUSEUMS AND GALLERIES

Oxford is fortunate, even for a university city, in its range of museums, several of which are of world-class quality. None of them resembles the dull and somewhat pathetic collection of isolated articles abandoned in dusty glass cases, which all of us will remember from our childhood. Instead, they are living reminders of man's cultural achievements and of his scientific prowess, all attractively arranged and periodically updated.

The Oxfordshire County Museum Service provides, free of charge, a most comprehensive guide to most of the museums and galleries in the city and county, and gives up-to-date details of opening times, leading treasures, and current displays and exhibitions, as well as indicating the facilities, such as shops, toilets or disabled access, which each has to offer. The guide is available in most museums, and in the Information Centre.

In addition to the more conventional or permanent museums and galleries, exhibitions are held in other venues such as the Long Room at New College, Halifax House Graduate Centre in South Parks Road, the Stables Gallery, Green College, and in the Exhibition Room at the Central Library in Westgate. The local press and publications such as *This Month in Oxford* should be consulted.

Not to be forgotten are the colleges' own treasures, some on display for the public to see. The best places to visit are the chapels for their stained glass – medieval, seventeenth-century, Pre-Raphaelite and modern – and for their portraits, statuary, brasses, silverwear and relics of great men. In addition, many dining halls are virtual picture galleries in their own right, showing members of the college from the founder down to the present Head of House.

Perhaps the single most renowned work of art in Oxford, however, is Keble College's copy of Holman Hunt's 'The Light of the World', which portrays Christ knocking on the door of the human heart. Keble's version is the original, but, when the College decided to display it in the chapel and charge for entry to view it, the artist was so furious that he set to and painted another copy. In fact there are three 'Lights of the World', and others being in St Paul's Cathedral, London, and in Manchester. The Oxford copy is still on display at Keble.

Ashmolean Museum
Beaumont Street

Open Tuesday to Saturday 10 a.m. to 4 p.m. Sundays 2 p.m. to 4 p.m. Bank Holiday Mondays 2 p.m. to 5 p.m. Closed other Mondays, Good Friday and Easter weekend, and the Monday and Tuesday of St Giles' Fair in early September.

The Ashmolean was founded in 1683, sixty years before the British Museum, and is therefore the oldest museum in the British Isles. The original building, still known as the Old Ashmolean, is now the Museum of the History of Science. The present one was built in the 1840s by Charles Cockerell, and housed the University Galleries. It was not until 1908 that the Art and Archaeological Collections were amalgamated.

The nucleus of the Museum's collections is the Tradescant Collection, donated by Elias Ashmole in 1678. It arrived in twelve cartloads, under the name of 'Tradescant's Ark'.

In 1776 the Ashmolean was raided by one John Peter Le Maitre, who made off with medals, coins and jewellery. He was later apprehended in Dublin, and as a punishment spent five years in the hulks. Le Maitre is better known as Jean Paul Marat, the French Revolutionary leader.

The Museum is divided up into sections, the principal ones being:

The Department of Western Art

The treasures here date from the fourteenth century, and comprise more than 1200 paintings. The department is particularly rich in Michelangelo drawings, which are housed in the Print Room, along with those of other Old Masters, such as Raphael. The fine collection of early Italian items were the gift of the Hon. W.T.H. Fox-Strangways.

The *Oxford Almanacs*, which still appear annually, go back to the eighteenth century, and are of great interest to those who wish to see Oxford buildings as they appeared in the past. The painter Turner of Oxford is also well represented.

Oxford was the home of the Pre-Raphaelite movement, many of whose members' masterpieces are on display in the Ashmolean. The French Impressionists, too, are in evidence, but it is the overall range of paintings, from medieval to modern which is most impressive.

Items in the department also include fine examples of European bronzes, musical instruments, jewellery, glass and ceramics from the Middle Ages onwards. In the McAlpine Gallery there is a series of changing exhibitions; see the posters on the museum gates for details.

The Department of Eastern Art

This department, opened in 1962, covers all aspects of art and archaeology of both the Near and Far East, from North Africa to

Japan. The collection includes exhibits from the former Indian Institute, and the department has its own library.

The Cast Gallery (1959)

This is in a new building, which adjoins the main museum. It contains casts of Greek and Roman sculpture and bronzes, and is used in the study of the classical world.

The Griffiths Institute

For Egyptological studies, this institute was founded in 1939. There is an impressive collection of Egyptian exhibits, from mummified cats to tombs, on the ground floor.

The Heberden Coin Room (1922)

Here there are coins, medals and tokens including most of those owned by the individual colleges. It is particularly strong on Greek, Roman, English and Oriental items.

The Department of Antiquities

These include not only Greek and Roman examples, but also some from the Middle East. Outstanding acquisitions are those from excavations carried out by Oxford men, notably Evans in Crete and Petrie in Egypt.

Exhibitions start with the Stone and Bronze Ages, and continue through the English Middle Ages and beyond, with special relics of important people.

Favourites include the Anglo-Saxon Alfred's jewel, possibly the star item in the whole museum, and those in the Founder's Room, a glorious hotch-potch of quaint and personal treasures, among which are Powhattan's mantle, Guy Fawkes's lantern, Cromwell's death-mask, and the iron-bound hat worn by Bradshaw when sentencing Charles I to death.

Tours of the Ashmolean are arranged and there is a club for junior enthusiasts.

Bate Collection of Historical Instruments
Faculty of Music, St Aldate's.

Open Monday to Friday 2 p.m. to 5 p.m.; closed occasionally during curator's absence.

Treasures include the Retford gift of bows, the Charles Taphouse collection of old keyboard instruments which is on permanent loan, and, the main attraction, one of only a couple or so complete Javanese gamelans in Britain. The gamelan is a percussion orchestra common in Indonesia, but rare in the western world.

Broad Canvas
20 Broad Street

Open usual shop hours.

This shop deals in everything an artist could possibly require. It also sells postcards, greetings cards and materials for other arts and crafts such as needlework and jewellery-making. Exhibitions are held on the first floor, and often specialize in views of Oxford by modern artists.

Chinese Arts Centre
50 High Street

Open usual shop hours.

Established in 1975, the centre deals with fine and applied arts. As well as original paintings and calligraphy, there is a large selection of reproductions for sale.

The gallery promotes and sells works by up-and-coming artists in China, and arranges exhibitions of their work in Britain, as well as cultural exchanges between the two countries.

Besides finished products, lovers of Chinese art can buy painting and calligraphy materials, jewellery, ceramics, books and magazines, kites, games, toys, records and cassettes.

Christ Church Picture Gallery
St Aldate's (or from Oriel Square)

Open Monday to Saturday 10.30 a.m. to 1 p.m. and 2 p.m. to 5.30 p.m. Sunday 2 p.m. to 5.30 p.m. Admission charge.

The college has its own collection of Old Masters, including Leonardo, some in a permanent exhibition. There are changing displays of Old Master drawings, mostly Italian, from the fourteenth to eighteenth centuries. In addition, there are special exhibitions.

Museum of Modern Art
30 Pembroke Street

Open Tuesday to Saturday 10 a.m. to 6 p.m. Sunday 2 p.m. to 6 p.m. Admission charge.

MoMA specializes in twentieth-century art of all kinds: photography, architecture and films as well as paintings. There are lectures, and even performances, and a changing programme of exhibitions, many featuring artists from the Third World or from Eastern Europe. There is a shop and a popular café.

Museum of the History of Science
Broad Street

Open Monday to Friday 10.30 a.m. to 1 p.m. and 2.30 p.m. to 4 p.m. Closed on Bank Holidays, and the weeks after Christmas and Easter. Also closed at certain times for academic use, for this is a teaching museum.

The Old Ashmolean Building which houses the Museum was constructed by the University to give a home to the collections made by Elias Ashmole, and to be used for lectures and as a chemical laboratory. The cost, including that of the site, was just over £4,500, and the building was opened in May 1683 in the presence of the Duke of York and the Princess Anne (later James II and Queen Anne).

In 1925 the important Lewis Evans collection of scientific instruments was donated to the University, and housed on the upper floor. By 1935, the museum's treasures had so much increased that it was decided to change its name from the Old Ashmolean to the Museum of the History of Science.

The highlights of the collections are:

Spheres, astrolabes, quadrants and sundials from medieval times until the nineteenth century.

Clocks and watches, many of them made in the city.

Astronomical instruments, particularly good-quality seventeenth and eighteenth-century items.

Optical instruments, microscopes and telescopes.

Einstein's blackboard, complete with his calculations.

Early apparatus for the teaching of physics and chemistry.

Early photographic equipment.

Medical and surgical instruments; anatomical preparations; equipment used in the production of penicillin in Oxford between 1939 and 1943.

Portraits of leading scientists.

Those who are not of a scientific turn of mind will still appreciate the beauty of the building itself, its furnishings and its décor.

Museum of Oxford
St Aldate's

Open Tuesday to Saturday 10 a.m. to 5 p.m.

Not at all the usual dreary type of town museum, but a series of exhibitions tracing life in Oxford from prehistoric to modern times, the museum shows how firstly the city, and then the University, evolved. Of great interest are the photographs and artists' impressions of medieval buildings, many of which were later incorporated into colleges and other structures; most of these survive, at least partially, today, but are not easily recognizable.

The visitor is taken through the centuries, from the legend of Oxford's patron saint, Frideswide, in cartoon form, through the city's golden age, with great monastic buildings, now lost forever, such as Osney Abbey, to the Renaissance, the Civil

War and the Seige of Oxford, when the capital was here. Next come the embryo Royal Society, the decline in Georgian times, and the second rebirth in the nineteenth century, ending with the age of the Morris motor-car, which was destined to change Oxford for ever. Older visitors will remember the type of shop fittings which have been brought from Cape's draper's shop when it closed its doors.

There are frequent temporary exhibitions on specific themes, and a shop.

The Oxford Story
Broad Street

Bookings and Information Office 33–5 George Street. Open daily throughout the year.

Conceived by Heritage Projects, the instigators of the Jorvik exhibition at York, the Oxford Story is staged in a former warehouse in the heart of the city. It opened in 1988 and initial teething-troubles led to the abandonment of the much-publicized 'medieval students' desks' in which visitors were to be whisked through time. Instead, one is provided with personal commentaries in a choice of languages, and guided through the three floors of displays which aim to bring to life not only the great men, women and events in the University's history, but also give an insight into modern Oxford. This journey starts with Friar Roger Bacon, in the thirteenth century, and one meets, among others, Wycliffe, Cranmer, Bodley, Charles I, Gladstone, Florey, and the present Chancellor of the University, Lord Jenkins, as Roy Jenkins, Balliol undergraduate.

The Oxfordshire and Buckinghamshire Light Infantry Regimental Museum
Territorial Army Centre, Slade Park, Headington, Oxford.

Check in advance for admission times.

This collection of uniforms, badges, medals and silver belongs to the County regiment, now part of the Royal Green Jackets.

The Pitt Rivers Museum
South Parks Road

Open Monday to Saturday 1 p.m. to 4.30 p.m.

Entered through the University Museum, the Pitt Rivers treasures were collected by General Pitt Rivers, and presented to the University in 1884. This is one of the world's most important museums of ethnology and prehistory, showing as it does the story of the world's chief arts and industries until the beginning of mass production. Outstanding items are the amulets and charms, weapons and armour, textiles and instruments, but most people will remember most clearly the totem, and the shrunken heads!

The Balfour Building, at 60 Banbury Road (open Monday to Saturday 1 p.m. to 4.30 p.m.) is part of the Pitt Rivers collection, specializing in musical instruments, of which it forms one of the largest collections anywhere, and exhibits featuring 'Hunters and Gatherers', past and present.

The Rotunda Museum of Antique Dolls' Houses
Grove House, Iffley Turn Oxford

Open either by written appointment, or on summer Sunday afternoons (May to mid-September) Admission charge. Note: no children under 16 admitted.

This collection of nearly fifty dolls' houses includes examples from 1700 to 1900, each with its own furnishings, crockery, silver, carpets, books and residents.

University Museum
Parks Road

Open Monday to Saturday 12 noon to 5 p.m. Closed Easter and Christmas weeks.

Second only to the British Museum's Natural History collections, the University Museum is much more than a showroom, being involved in a great deal of undergraduate teaching, reference and research.

The zoological collections include preserved specimens from all over the world, some of them being a hundred years old.

The Hope Entomological Collections, presented in 1849 – a Hope Professorship was endowed in 1861 – form the basis of exhibits which have been augmented by many subsequent collections of insects, with a strong bias towards spiders.

The geological collections have fine specimens of Jurassic vertebrates, as well as Palaeozoic and Pleistocene collections.

The mineral collections include more than 20,000 specimens, and are leaders among provincial museum exhibits.

The building itself, high Victorian with columns made of many different types of British stone and rock, and a glass roof, is most individual, and has associations with John Ruskin in his unsuccessful attempts at becoming an amateur architect!

It should be noted that several of Oxford's museums are closed on Mondays and plans made accordingly. Similarly, certain sections, and, indeed, in some cases, the entire museum may be closed due to its use for teaching or research purposes, so it is sensible to check in advance if the visit is of importance to your trip.

Music in Oxford

The Heather Professorship of Music was founded in 1626, but England had become the centre of European music, in the time of Elizabeth I, with Oxford a centre of English music. The University produced early composers such as Morley and Dowland, and by the seventeenth century music-making was very popular, as Anthony à Wood was able to record in his *Diary* on many occasions. Wood himself attended weekly meetings, and the University Musical Club met on Tuesday evenings.

The eighteenth century carried on this tradition, and Handel's concerts in the Sheldonian attracted a record audience of an estimated 3,700. This was in 1733, when *Athelia* made its debut, and the composer gave five concerts in all, charging for entrance and thus establishing the tradition of public performances in Britain.

The University 'Act' or degree ceremony had always been an event in which music played an important part, usually performed by local artistes, as Thomas Hearne jealously recorded when he referred to the newcomer, Handel, as being supported by a 'lousy Crew' of 'forreign fiddlers'.

In 1791 Haydn received an honorary Doctorate in Music, and, for his 'thesis', wrote a piece which read the same forwards as backwards. His *Oxford Symphony* was written in recognition of his honour.

The next century, however, proved a period in which music was looked on as a luxury and an unnecessary distraction from the more serious things in life, such as studying and religion, although there was a renaissance towards the middle of the century. Since then, practically every great name in the world of music has either performed in Oxford or been awarded an honorary D. Mus. Honorands include Vaughan Williams, Rostropovich, Shostakovitch, Yehudi Menuhin, Paderewski, Segovia, and, more recently, Kiri Te Kanawa, Pierre Boulez, Bernard Haitinck and Sir Geraint Evans.

Today Oxford is truly a city of music, as concerts and recitals are held all over the town throughout the year. First-class concerts are given by world-class performers, principally in the Sheldonian Theatre, where a four-day long music festival was held during its opening ceremonies in July 1669. Other venues are the Town Hall, the Apollo Theatre, the Cathedral, the University Church and Holywell Music Room, the oldest in Europe, opened in 1749. Top-line opera companies, such as the Welsh and Scottish National, and the D'Oyly Carte, visit the Apollo Theatre regularly.

Recitals are held frequently in the college libraries and chapels, and in the Maison Française, Norham Road, during term time. Many colleges have their own music societies, and there is a University Orchestra, as well as the Oxford Philharmonic and similar societies.

At the Music Faculty, in St Aldate's, is the Bate Collection of

Musical Instruments, open to the public (see page 190).

Lastly, but certainly not least, are the three choir schools at New College, Christ Church and Magdalen, all of which broadcast, record and go on tour regularly, as well as singing in their respective chapels and holding concerts.

For those who prefer rock and pop, modern music performers appear at the Apollo Theatre, at the Polytechnic, and at the colleges' summer balls. On a more informal level, talented buskers are to be heard in the city streets, usually in Queen Street, Cornmarket and the Covered Market, at Christmas and during the summer months.

Promoters

It should be noted that tickets for concerts can be obtained either from the promoters direct, from Blackwell's Music Shop in Holywell Street, or from the Tickets in Oxford bureau in the Information Centre, St Aldate's. They are only available from the venues themselves on the night of the performance, in most cases, the obvious exception being the Apollo Theatre.

The Bach Choir
Box Office Secretary, PO Box 326, Oxford OX2 6UN

Formed in 1896, the choir is based in the Sheldonian Theatre, where it gives at least two concerts each year. It has many undergraduate members among the 200-strong ranks, but is distinctly Town and Gown in its membership, some of which is drawn from the more distant parts of the Thames Valley.

Originally the Bach Choir performed mainly classical choral works, but now its repertoire includes the moderns as well. The choir has performed the works of such great composers as Vaughan Williams, Holst and Walton in their presence. A past Bach Choir member, Mr Edward Heath, the former Prime Minister, has appeared as guest conductor at their concerts.

Music at Oxford
6a Cumnor Hill, Oxford OX2 9HA (0865 864056)

The leading promoter of music in the county, Music at Oxford specializes in baroque concerts, although they also engage international orchestras, and more specialist groups.

Concerts are held at least weekly, often more frequently, highlights being the 'Handel In Oxford' Festival in early July, and the series of Promenade Concerts which run to teddy bears' picnics, and Twenties-style events.

Music at Oxford venues are the Sheldonian Theatre, the Holywell Music Room, Christ Church Cathedral, the University Church, St Cross Church, the Town Hall, the Apollo Theatre and, further afield, Dorchester Abbey and Nuneham Park.

City of Oxford Orchestra
11–12 Cornmarket Street, Oxford OX1 3EX (0865   24035)

Formerly known as Oxford Pro Musica, the Orchestra's performances include the Oxford Subscription Concerts which date from 1920. These were originally mainly philharmonic and symphony orchestral, gradually including more and more recitals. Today these are the most usual type of concert, and are of a world-class standard, ranging from Bach to Bernstein. Some include pre-concert talks. Venues include the Sheldonian Theatre, the Apollo Theatre, Christ Church Cathedral, and the Town Hall.

DRAMA IN OXFORD
The University theatre, the Playhouse, in Beaumont Street, has built up an international reputation for itself; sadly, its future is uncertain, due to lack of funding. It is now closed as a full-time theatre, only opening on occasions for the presentation of the Oxford University Dramatic Society, the OUDS, pronounced 'Owds'.

The Playhouse began life in 1923 in a house in the Woodstock

Road. This subsequently collapsed some six years later, and the present building, which was designed by Sir Edward Maufe, dates from the 1930s. The seating capacity is around 673, and all student drama societies, whether at University or college level, have a right to put on productions there.

In the 1940s, the Playhouse saw the acting debut of the young Richard Burton, then an undergraduate at Exeter College. Burton never forgot his beginnings, and, together with Elizabeth Taylor, helped the theatre in many ways, even financing an extension named the Burton Rooms.

The Apollo Theatre, George Street, Oxford OX1 2AG (0865 244544/5) as has already been stated, is a major venue for concerts of all kinds. Other performances include musicals, comedies, drama and the annual pantomime, in which nationally famous stars appear.

The Pegasus Theatre, in Magdalen Road (0865 722851) is the home of the Oxford Youth Theatre, and, as such, offers a less traditional type of entertainment, with works by up-and-coming playwrights.

Throughout the year plays are performed in various college halls, and in the Union Building in St Michael's Street. Towards the end of Trinity Term, the college drama societies put on productions out of doors in the college gardens; coats, macs, and travelling-rugs are strongly recommended!

EATING AND DRINKING IN HISTORICAL SURROUNDINGS

The unadventurous eater, in search of the proverbial good plain cooking, is likely to be dismayed in Oxford, not by the quality of the food, but by the sheer range on offer.

Of course there are some pubs which serve up little more than the obligatory pie and chips and ploughman's lunches, but the vast majority of Oxford's eating-places vie with each other in providing something both satisfying and unusual, such as steak and Guinness casserole, or gamekeeper's pie, in addition to French, Italian or Mexican dishes of the day.

Not surprisingly, Oxford has its fair share of the so-called 'ethnic' restaurants, mainly Chinese and Indian, concentrated in the Cowley Road and Jericho areas. There are also plenty of wine-bars, bistros, and coffee-shops.

For a genuinely Oxford experience, however, at least one lunch time should be spent in one of the more historical of the city's eateries, most of which are public houses. The outsider may be persuaded that some of them are crowded and noisy, and their clientele a little pretentious, at least in term time, but at least he or she will be able to recognize them when they next appear in a documentary, film or novel. Certain places have become an almost essential part of the Oxford scenery.

The following are perhaps the top ten in historical eating places, although, naturally enough, everyone has a particular favourite.

'The Bear', Alfred Street, was once an important coaching inn. That part of it which survives was once the rooms used by the ostlers. 'The Bear' is known for its collection of ties from all over the world. Cut off below the knot, they come from clubs, societies, schools and universities, and the collection, which has reached about 7,500 specimens, is displayed in glass cases on the pub walls.

'The Bulldog', St Aldate's. Look for the pub's sign which shows the traditional British canine on one side, while on the reverse may be seen the Oxford version of the word, a bowler-hatted University constable in hot pursuit of an erring student. 'The Bulldog' has been known to display its menu outside the front door written in several languages, including Japanese.

'The Chequers', off High Street. Tucked away down a medieval alleyway, this city-centre pub has a collection of translations of its own title in dozens of languages and a variety of alphabets.

'The Eagle and Child', otherwise known as the 'Bird and Baby', St Giles Street. This former haunt of C.S. Lewis and J.R.R. Tolkien in the 1950s, where their club, the 'Inklings' used to meet, has recently been refurbished to give an idea of how it would have appeared to them at this time.

'The King's Arms', corner of Holywell and South Parks Road. This former coaching inn belongs to Wadham College, and has the flat where the University Verger resides, above the pub itself. 'The King's Arms' is very much a University affair, and was once notorious in feminist circles for its 'Men Only' Bar.

'The Mitre', High Street, is possibly the best-known of Oxford's hostelries, having appeared in poems, novels, broadsheets and memoires for centuries. The present rather Dickensian frontage dates from the 1630s in part, the rest being later seventeenth-century or more recent still. The rib-vaulted cellar, however, formerly known as Monk's Retreat and used for an additional bar and venue for a folk club, goes back to the thirteenth century. The former hotel rooms have names, and at least one of them is said to be haunted.

Today, the first two floors of 'The Mitre' are open to the public, as it is now a Berni Inn, the décor and fare being unmistakably so, while the upper part is used by the owners, Lincoln College, for student accommodation. The Old Mitre Rooms, in Turl Street, are available during the Long Vacation as hotel rooms; for details, contact Lincoln College.

'The Nosebag', 6-8 St Michael's Street, is not a pub, although it is licensed, and sells drinks such as cider. Situated over the old city wall, it has oak beams, pine furniture and Laura Ashley décor.

'The Perch', Binsey Lane, off Botley Road, is one of the places to go on a summer evening. As its name suggests it stands by the river, near Port Meadow, and is thatched, with large gardens where Lewis Caroll gave some of the first readings of *Alice*.

'The Trout', 195 Godstow Road, Wolvercote. Another riverside pub suitable for long, light evenings, when one can sit and watch the weir and listen to the peacocks, 'The Trout' is equally attractive in the winter when its open fires and low ceiling make it into a perfect haunt for the ghost of a naval officer which is said to place its order, and then disappear.

'The Turf Tavern', Bath Place, off Holywell, or down St Helen's Passage, off New College Lane. The future of this medieval pub, which nestles against the ancient city wall, under the wing of New College, seems assured now, after a legal wrangle which disputed the terms of the will of a former host. During the time that 'The Turf' was closed, Oxford waited anxiously for news of this well-known attraction.

THE OXFORD YEAR

Anybody who spends a length of time in Oxford with connections with the University will have to get into the habit of thinking of the year as starting in October, and finishing with the Long Vacation.

It is slightly more difficult to attempt to think in weeks of term, rather than in months of the year. For instance, 'the Wednesday of 7th Week of Trinity' translates as 7 June; similarly, an Oxford periodical dates its first edition of the term as '0th Week'.

Luckily, the three Oxford Terms, Michaelmas, Hilary and Trinity, only last eight weeks each, and so the brain is not severely over-taxed. One can always cheat and look in the University diary.

Oxford is the home of many traditions, some of them centuries old, others fairly recent in origin, or revived. Some of these are known all over the English-speaking world, but others are of riveting interest only to the college or individuals concerned.

Michaelmas Term

October: First Saturday morning of term, in mid-month, Matriculation, held in the Sheldonian Theatre.
Last week of October, or the first week in November, bonfire

and firework parties, the most spectacular of which is held in South Park.

Christmas and New Year: Carol service in Christ Church Cathedral.
Boar's Head Ceremony at the Queen's College.
Christmas pantomimes and other seasonal productions.
Mummers' plays at the Headington pubs, usually Boxing Day morning.
New Year's Day Needle and Thread Ceremony at the Queen's College.

Hilary Term

January: On 14 January, in the first year of every century, the Hunting of the Mallard at All Souls College.
February: Bumps races on the Thames, 'Torpids'.
March: Installation of the Proctors in Convocation House.
University Boat Race with Cambridge (may be early April).

Trinity Term

May: May Morning (1 May) hymn-singing from Magdalen Tower, Morris dancing. Eights Week, late in the month.
Late Spring Bank Holiday: Lord Mayor's Parade and fête in South Park.
Ascension Day: Beating of the bounds of the parish of St Michael-at-the-North Gate.
Corpus Christi Day: Procession round Magdalen cloisters, followed by a service in the chapel.
June: Tortoise Fair in Corpus Christi College garden.
Final examinations, start late May and continue into July.
College balls take place over several weeks.

The Long Vacation

June: Last Wednesday in the month, Lord Crewe's Benefaction and Encaenia. Sunday after the 24th, open air sermon preached from pulpit in Magdalen College, in honour of St John the Baptist.

Music in Oxford Handel Festival (runs into July); also features other leading composers. Ten or so days of concerts in the Sheldonian Theatre, and in the grounds of Nuneham Park, outside Oxford.

July: Sheriff's races and other entertainment on Port Meadow.

September: first Monday and Tuesday after the first Sunday, St Giles' Fair, a very large fun-fair stretching from Magdalen Street, past St Giles. Expect traffic diversions and closed buildings.

SOME OXFORD VILLAGES

Binsey

The hamlet of Binsey is approached by car down the Botley Road, past the station, and then along Binsey Lane. On foot one may get there either along the towpath by the side of Osney Bridge, or across Port Meadow.

Although there is little more to Binsey than a couple of farms and cottages round a village green, besides the well-known 'Perch' public house, it is, nevertheless, one of the places to go if spending a period of time in Oxford during the summer months.

Binsey church, dedicated to St Margaret of Antioch, is about half a mile north-west of the hamlet itself, and is reached along an avenue of chestnut trees. In the churchyard is St Margaret's Well, said to be the spot where St Frideswide struck the ground in order that a healing spring should appear for Prince Algar to bathe his eyes and restore his sight.

The steps down to the well were given by the Reverend Thomas Prout in 1874, and a tablet there commemorates the gift. The well water, said to be beneficial to those with eye complaints, even to this day, is the origin of the 'Treacle Well', joking references to which so caught the imagination of Lewis Carroll that he introduced it into the conversation at the Mad Hatter's tea party. The word treacle, is, in fact, derived from 'theriaca', Latin for antidote, because of its healing powers.

The church itself, which dates from the twelfth century, consists of chancel, nave and belfry only, and it is this very simplicity which is in itself attractive. Furnishings include the painted arms of Queen Anne, a tub-shaped font, probably twelfth-century, and a carving of St Frideswide by Eric Gill, hidden away on the inside of the pulpit because it has a knot of wood in a rather inconvenient place!

Cowley

Cowley is synonymous world-wide with the motor industry, and the influence of the second William Morris is evident everywhere in this, his home village. He went to the parish school, moved into Oxford's Longwall Street to repair and then make bicycles, and went back to Cowley to start up a car factory in the former Military College there. His first car appeared in 1911, and by 1921 he was able to mass-produce models which became so popular that the Cowley boy became a millionaire and one of the most munificent of Oxford's benefactors.

Although Cowley has all the usual trappings of consumer society: the Austin-Rover works, a draughty shopping-centre, and roads and roads of semi-detached houses, it also has a conservation area. This lies around St James's church in Beauchamp Lane, from which there is a view over all the towers and spires of Oxford.

The church has a late twelfth-century font and chancel arch, and a squat tower, three centuries younger, with gargoyles, but which was virtually rebuilt by Street between 1862 and 1865. In 1864 the architect raised the height of the church roof, hence the squat appearance of the tower, and added a new north aisle. This somewhat drastic rebuilding saved St James's from demolition, for it had been condemned as being too small for the rapidly growing congregation.

A new church, St Luke's, on the main Oxford Road, was the gift of William Morris.

Oxford Road, Cowley, becomes Cowley Road, Oxford as it nears the city. En route, up a lane between Southfield Road and Bartlemas Close, is St Bartholomew's Chapel. This is all that remains of a hospital founded by Henry I, probably as a lazar-house; the main buildings lay to the north of the chapel. It was rebuilt by Oriel College in 1649, and its external appearance altered considerably. St Bartholomew's Farmhouse nearby is sixteenth-century.

Headington

The Headington area was settled by the Romans, as we know from their kilns found on the Churchill Hospital site. There is a Roman bath at Wick Farm, about a mile west of Barton Estate. Dating from about 1660 is the well-house, small, square, and made of stone, with an ogee dome, and topped by a lion's face which acts as key-stone. Inside is a stone seat, and steps leading down to the covered well.

A Saxon manor was first mentioned in 1004 when its tithes were granted by Ethelred the Unready to St Frideswide's Priory, later to become the Cathedral. It is noted once again in 'Domesday Book' of 1086.

During the Civil War, Headington served as a look-out post for Parliamentarian forces, spying on Royalist Oxford at the bottom of Headington Hill. In the course of the eighteenth and nineteenth centuries, middle- and upper-class building develop-ment gradually surrounded the old, stone-built heart of the village, centred on St Andrew's church and 'The White Hart' public house.

St Andrew's, the parish church of Old Headington, has a chancel arch built around 1160, and a fifteenth-century chancel. The roof has recently been restored and repainted in bright, medieval colours, and there are old pictures, medieval tiles, and other relics on show from the church's past. In the churchyard are interesting tombs and gravestones, going back to the mid-seventeenth century, and an ancient preaching-cross which was given a new top in the 1960s.

The picturesque lane of cottages known as the Croft, running between Old High Street and Osler Road, once acted as a sort of service road for the larger houses in St Andrew's Road. In all, some thirty-three properties in Old Headington are listed buildings.

Headington House, completed in 1783, was built for William Jackson, the printer of *Jackson's Oxford Journal*; today it is occupied by Sir Isaiah Berlin.

Beside Old Headington there is also New Headington, which has its own High Street and parish church, as does Headington Quarry, where, from the fifteenth to the nineteenth centuries, much of the stone used in Oxford buildings was quarried. There are still some stone-workers' cottages in Quarry, and all sort of indentations where quarrying has taken place over the years.

Headington is the home of Morris dancing, ancient and modern, for it was here, at a house on the London Road, where Horwood Close now stands, that Cecil Sharp saw his first Morris men, on Boxing Day 1899. So lasting was the impact that he achieved a revival in folk-dance and song, nationwide. Headington has named a close of houses after him, unfortunately wrongly spelled, for they have added an 'e' to his surname.

On London Road, which runs towards the A40 and joins the three Headingtons, are Oxford Polytechnic and the Manor, Oxford United Football Club's ground, opposite which, in New High Street, is Oxford's most recent tourist attraction – a terraced house with an enormous fibre-glass shark plunging through its roof.

Iffley

One may get to Iffley either by car or bus along the Iffley Road, which is the third exit from the Plain on leaving the city centre, or on foot along the towpath from Folly Bridge, some two miles.

On the Thames, a couple of miles south-east of Oxford,

modern Iffley is a suburb, while remaining in many ways a place apart. It is this feeling of separateness which is the charm of the older part of the village, little affected by the housing developments of its near neighbours, Cowley and Rose Hill.

Apart from recently built roads and closes, Iffley consists of one long main street, flanked by low stone houses and cottages, some of them thatched and a few dating back to the Middle Ages. One such building is the thatched school-house, south of the church, which started life as a barn and was promoted to the position of parish school in 1838. Opposite is its predecessor, the Dame School, which bears the inscription 'Mrs Sarah Nowell's School 1822'. The rectory incorporates some twelfth-century work, plus many other reminders of the medieval builders. It is a gabled, stone-built place, with diamond-shaped brick chimneys and a red-tiled roof.

It is St Mary's church, however, which is Iffley's main attraction, featuring in many a work on architecture as one of the country's best examples of a Norman church (see page 100).

Court Place has the date 1580 on the wall facing the church, but its fabric is mainly Georgian. The Malt House has a fourteenth-century window built into its barn, and a stone figure of a bishop is probably seventeenth-century.

Jericho

This former working-class suburb, which stretches from Walton Street westwards to the canal, is made up of a warren of little streets. Its terraced cottages were built to house workers at the Oxford University Press nearby, and other early residents included railway workers, artisans, and minor craftsmen. The Victorian Census Returns show a surprisingly varied selection of occupations and birthplaces. These same cottages are today very desirable residences for students, lecturers and professional people.

The parish church of St Barnabas, in Cardigan Street, was financed, at a cost of £6,500, by an early patron of the Pre-Raphaelite brotherhood, Thomas Combe, in 1869. It was designed by Blomfield in an Italian Romanesque style, with Gothic details, and a campanile which was added in 1872, at a further cost of £800, and later re-roofed.

'Barnie' church features in *Jude the Obscure* as 'St Silas's'; Thomas Hardy would have been well acquainted with the church for he worked upon it as an architectural assistant, and used Jericho as a setting for the district in which Jude first settles in Oxford, which he calls 'Beersheba'.

CONCLUSION

Few people who are familiar with both Oxford and Oxfordshire will agree on what it means to them, particularly Oxford itself. Different people see different aspects, depending on their own personal preferences.

Samuel Pepys, for example, a Cambridge man himself, considered Oxford 'a very sweet place, Oxford, a mighty fine place and well seated and cheap entertainment' in 1668. Horace Walpole, on the other hand, was to write in 1751, of 'that nursery of nonsense and bigotry, Oxford'. Even Lewis Carroll found that 'Nothing *ever* happens here, I believe! There never *was* such a place for things not happening', whereas Swinburne put it a little more strongly when he declared that people in Oxford could not be said to die 'for they never begin to live'. It was Matthew Arnold, though, Oxford's Professor of Poetry, who gave us what has become the classic cameo of 'that sweet city with her dreaming spires', a vision which has endured, if mistakenly, to this day, even though Hardy's Jude was much more taken with Oxford's atmosphere of medieval decay.

In 1903 Shaw put it most non-committally: 'a very nice sort of place, Oxford, I should think, for people who like that sort of place', but, by 1938, Margaret Halsey found that, 'from a purely tourist standpoint, Oxford is overpowering, being so replete with architecture and history and anecdote that the visitor's mind feels dribbling and helpless, as with an over-large mouthful of nougat'.

W.H. Auden, a Christ Church man, did not beat about the bush; 'Oxford city is sheer hell. Compared with New York it's five times as crowded and the noise of the traffic is six times louder. Ironically enough, I had to leave New York and come to Oxford in order to get robbed.'

One speaks as one finds, but, like Jan Morris, most of us periodically give thanks that we are lucky enough 'to be grumbling there at all'. The majority of Oxford's thousands of visitors, thankfully, agree, and pay millions of dollars and other currencies for the privilege.

Perhaps the last word on Oxford should be given to Flora Thompson, born in 1876 near Cottisford, Oxfordshire. In her autobiographical *Lark Rise to Candleford* she makes the child, Laura, ask her aunt what Oxford is like. 'Well, it's all old buildings, churches and colleges where rich people's sons go to school when they're grown up', answers Aunt Jenny. A little girl from Lark Rise, who had stayed there in her aunt's university lodging-house, and various other villagers' reports combined to build up for Laura a 'dim blur of bishops ... and swings, and shows and coconut-shies and little girls sucking pink-and-white rock and polishing shoes. To imagine a place without pigsties and vegetable gardens was more difficult. With no bacon or cabbage, what could people have to eat?'

It is easy enough for us to laugh at such naïvety from those who lived a mere nineteen miles from Oxford, but to me, at least, the most curious thing of all about Oxfordshire is the fact that very, very few people indeed not connected with the University, even those who live within the city boundaries, either know, or have any desire to know, anything about one of the most fascinating cities in the world.

BIBLIOGRAPHY

Betjeman, Sir John, *An Oxford University Chest*, Oxford University Press 1979

Bodleian Library, *The Bodleian Library Oxford*

Chapter House of Christ Church Oxford, *A Concise Guide to the Colleges of Oxford University*, 8th edition 1984

Colvin, H.M., *The Sheldonian Theatre and Divinity School*, Oxford University Press 1981

Madan, Falconer, *Oxford Outside the Guide Books*, Blackwell 1923

Mee, Arthur, ed., *The King's England, Oxfordshire*, Hodder & Stoughton 1942

Morris, Jan, *Oxford*, Oxford University Press 1978

Oxford Times Newspaper, *Limited Edition* Magazine, issued monthly

Patterson-Ellis, W., *Jackson's Oxford Journal*, manuscript extracts, in Bodleian Library

Pevsner, N., and Sherwood, J., *Oxfordshire*, The Buildings of England Series, Penguin 1975

University of Oxford, *Calendar*, Oxford University Press, annually

    Campaign for Oxford, Oxford Development Office 1988

    Graduate Studies Prospectus, annually

    Oxford University Handbook

    Oxford University Information Office Fact Sheet

    Oxford University Information Office: Oxford University and its Colleges

    University of Oxford Historical Register to 1900, Oxford University Press 1900

University of Oxford Undergraduate Prospectus, Oxford University Press, annually

Venables, D.R., and Clifford, R.E., *Academic Dress of the University of Oxford*, 6th edition, Oxford 1985

Wood, Anthony, *The Life and Times*, Oxford University Press, World's Classics 1961

Yurdan, Marilyn, *Oxfordshire and Oxford*, Shire Publications 1988

INDEX